I0428987

In Nesting Time

by Olive Thorne Miller

Copyright © 4/7/2016
Jefferson Publication

ISBN-13: 978-1530948994

Printed in the United States of America

Table of Contents

BABY BIRDS.

And oft an unintruding guest,
I watched her secret toils from day to day;
How true she warped the moss to form the nest,
And modeled it within with wood and clay.
And by and by, like heath-bells gilt with dew,
There lay her shining eggs as bright as flowers,
Ink-spotted over, shells of green and blue:
And there I witnessed in the summer hours
A brood of Nature's minstrels chirp and fly,
Glad as the sunshine and the laughing sky.
John Clare.

I.

BABY BIRDS.

"Ears have they, but they hear not," may be said of all the world. Tragedies and comedies go on continually before us which we neither see nor hear; cries of distress and prattle of infants, songs of love and screams of war, alike fall upon deaf ears, while we calmly discuss the last book or the news from Borriboo-lah-Gha, as completely oblivious as if all this stirring life did not exist.

To be sure these things take place in the "upper stories," as Thoreau says, but they are none the less audible, and one is tempted to believe that bird voices are on a scale to which the untrained ear is not attuned. Once learn to hear, and nature is full of life and interest. The home affairs of our little neighbors whose modest cottage swings on a branch of the elm beside the door are more attractive than those of our fellow creatures in the house across the way partly because they are so open in their lives that our attentions do not seem intrusive, but more because their ways are not so familiar. We can guess how men and women pass their time, but we cannot guess why the cat-bird always sings from the middle of one particular shrub, nor where he has hidden his dusky spouse and nest full of babies; and after we know him we are eager to discover.

Upon reaching the charming home of a friend in Massachusetts last June, almost the first thing I saw was a pair of purple crow blackbirds in trouble. First arose a medley of queer husky tones, clamorous baby cries, and excited oriole voices, with violent agitation of the leaves of a tall elm, ending with the sudden exit of a blackbird, closely followed by a pair of Baltimore orioles. The pursued flew leisurely across the lawn, plainly in no haste, and not at all with the air of the thief and nest robber he is popularly supposed to be. Clearly the elm belonged by bird custom to the orioles, for their pretty swinging hammock could be seen partly hidden by leaves, about halfway up the tree, and what business other than that of marauder had the sombre-hued enemy upon it?

Now the blackbird has no secrets in his life; the whole world is welcome to know his affairs, and in fact he proclaims them loudly himself. It was easy to see that he had anxiety enough of his own just then, without thinking of disturbing his neighbors, for he was engaged in the task of introducing his young family to the world, and every bird watcher knows that is attended with almost as many difficulties as is the same operation in what we call "society."

If the youngster escape the dangers peculiar to the nest, the devouring jaws of squirrel or owl, the hands of the egg thief, being shaken out by the wind, smothered by an intrusive cow-bunting, or orphaned by the gun of a "collector;" if, neither stolen, eaten, thrown out, nor starved, he arrives at the age that his wings begin to stir and force him out of the leafy green tent of his birth, a new set of dangers meet him at the door. He may entangle himself in a hair of the nest-lining, and hang himself at the very threshold of life—a not uncommon occurrence; or he may safely reach the nearest twig and from there fall and break his neck—not a rare accident; he may be attacked by a bird who questions his right to be on the tree; he may fly, and, not reaching his goal, come to the ground, an easy prey to any prowler.

4

In this blackbird family one of the little ones had taken his first ambitious flight to the oriole's tree, where he must and should be fed and comforted, in spite of the hostile reception of its gayly dressed proprietor. The father took upon himself this duty, and many times during the day the above-mentioned scene was reënacted, loud blackbird calls, husky baby notes, the musical war-cry of the oriole, and a chase.

A second infant had wisely confined his wandering to his own tree, one of a group of tall pines that towered above the roofs of the village. This one could be easily watched as he stood on one branch for an hour at a time, sometimes in the nest attitude, head sunk in shoulders and beak pointed toward the sky, again looking eagerly around on his new world, turning his head from side to side, changing position to see the other way, and showing himself wide awake although the yellowish baby-down was still on his head, and his tail was not an inch long. Now and then the mother was heard calling in the distance, and as she approached he became all excitement, fluttering his wings, and answering in the husky tones of the family. A moment later, after a quick glance around, but without alighting and reconnoitring the whole neighborhood, as the robin does, she came down beside the eager youngling, administered to the wide open mouth what looked like two or three savage pecks, but doubtless were nothing worse than mouthfuls of food, and instantly flew again, while the refreshed infant stretched his wings and legs, changed his place a little, and settled into comfortable quiet after his lunch.

The urchin in the enemy's tree was not the most unfortunate of the nestlings. One already lay dead on the ground under the nest where it had fallen, and another came down during the day, though happily without injury. This one was not very bright, or perhaps his baby wits were dazed by his sudden descent. He made no objection to staying in my hand as long as I liked to look at him, and when I placed him on a low branch, as a hint that it was safer there, he declined to accept my advice, but flew off and came to the ground again. He was a scraggy looking, rusty black little fellow, the most unattractive young bird I ever saw. Shortly after this he clambered up on a pile of brush about a foot high, without so much as a leaf to screen him, and there he stayed all day, motionless, being fed at long intervals; and there I left him at night, never expecting to see him again. But in the morning he appeared on a low shrub on the lawn, and about nine o'clock he took courage to launch himself on wing. He flew very low across the street, and dropped into the tall grass at the foot of a lilac bush. Why the parents considered that less safe than the open lawn I could not see, but they evidently did, for one of them perched upon the lilac, and filled the air with anxious "chucks," announcing to all whom it might concern—after the fashion of some birds—that here was a stray infant to be had for the picking up. Perhaps, however, the hue-and-cry kept off the quiet-loving cat; at any rate nothing happened to him, I think, for in a day or two the three young birds became so expert on wing that the whole family left us, and I hope found a place where they were more welcome than in that colony of house and orchard birds.

Not so quiet in their ways are the babies of another blackbird family—the redwings; restless and uneasy, the clumsy little creatures climb all about the bushes and trees, and keep both parents busy, not only in filling their gaping mouths, but in finding them when the food is brought. They are always seeking a new place, and from the moment of leaving the nest show in a marked way the unrest, the impatience of the redwing family.

Quite as erratic is a much smaller bird, the yellow throated warbler, whose baby ways I have seen at the South. One of these bantlings no bigger than the end of a thumb will easily keep its parent frantically busy rushing about after food, and hunting up the capricious wanderer on its return.

The wood thrush, on the contrary, is patience itself. A youngster of this lovely family sits a half hour at a time motionless and silent on a branch, head drawn down upon his shoulders, apparently in the deepest meditation. When he sees food coming he is gently agitated, rises upon his weak legs, softly flutters his wings and opens his mouth, but never—never cries. Should one put a hand down to take him, as seemingly could be done easily, he will slip out from under it, drop to the ground, and disappear, in perfect silence.

The cry-baby of the bird world is the Baltimore oriole. As soon as this fluffy young person appears outside of his nursery, sometimes even before, he begins to utter a strange almost constant "chrr-r-r." He is not particularly active of movement, but he cannot keep silent. One little oriole mother whom I watched in Massachusetts had no help in raising her brood, her mate spending his time on the upper branches of the tree. He could not be blamed, however; he was, so far as I could see, perfectly willing to aid in the support of the family, but Madam actually would not allow him even to visit the homestead. When the young were out he assumed his share of the labor. The first yellow-haired bairn mounted the edge of the nest one morning, and after a little stretching and pluming, tried to fly. But alas he was held! Two or three times he renewed the attempt, his struggles always ending in failure, and I feared I should see a tragedy. Half an hour later the mother returned, and whether she pushed him down, or merely advised him to go back and try again, I cannot say. The fact is that he did disappear in the nest, where he remained for two or three hours, for it is probably safe to assume that the urchin who came up later was the same. This time, without delay upon the brink, he climbed upon a twig, hopped about a little, and before long flew several feet, alighting on a small branch of the same tree. Hardly had he established himself safely and resumed his ordinary call, when down upon him from above came a robin, who, strange to say, had a nest in one of the upper branches of the same tall maple. This robin had always recognized the right of the oriole parents to their share of the tree, but the young one was a stranger, and he fell upon him accordingly. He knocked him off his perch; the unfortunate little fellow fell a few feet, then gathered himself, fluttered and caught at the outside of a clump of leaves on the end of a twig, where after frantic struggling he managed to secure a hold. Perhaps the robin saw his mistake, for he paid no more attention to the new-comer, who did not stay long on the tree after this second disaster.

The next morning came up out of the nest quite an unnatural oriole baby—he did not cry. Silently, he stepped out upon a twig, and looked about in the new world around him. He carefully dressed his feathers, and often rose to his full height and stretched his legs, as if it were legs and not wings he needed in his new life. The third scion of the household had also a marked character of his own. Having planted himself on the threshold, and found it a convenient place to intercept all food on its way to the younger ones still unseen, he remained. Every time the mother came with a mouthful, he fluttered and coaxed, and usually got it. It was too good a situation to leave and he seemed to have settled for life; but his wings overpowered his inertia or greed, about four o'clock in the afternoon.

So long had the third young oriole occupied his position, that the fourth made his appearance almost immediately, as though he had been waiting. There does appear to be some regulation of this sort among the orioles, for in all that I have noticed, no two ever came out together (excepting once, when both went back almost instantly, and one returned alone). This late comer had not the whole long sunny day to loiter away, and he flew in an hour. The fifth and last came up early the next morning evidently in haste to join the scattered family, for he bade farewell to the native tree in a short time. No more orioles appeared upon the maple from this day, but for two weeks I saw the little party about; the father, whom I had missed after the flight of the first infant, working like a drudge, with two or three hungry urchins wherever he went, excepting when he sought food in the new-cut grass on the ground. He gave us no more songs, but his sweet, low call sounded all day on the place.

Another family of little folk came upon the maple after the orioles were gone, a nuthatch tribe. There were three or four of them exactly like the mother excepting a shorter tail, and they followed her like a flock of sheep, over and under branches, around the trunk, up or down or any way, never pausing more than an instant, not even when she plumped a morsel into a waiting mouth. She led her little procession by her querulous-sounding "quank," while they replied with a low "chir-up" in the same tone. It was a very funny sight. They could fly nicely, but never seemed to think of looking for food, and it was plain that the busy little mother had no time to teach them. It was interesting to see her deal with a moth which she found napping on a fence. She ran at once to a crack or some convenient hole in the rough rail, thrust it in and hammered it down. When it was quiet she snipped off the wings, dragged it out, and beat it on the fence till it was fit for food, the family meanwhile gathered around her, clinging closely to the fence, and gently fluttering. These nuthatches were remarkably silent, but some that I once saw living near the top of two or three tall pines were quite noisy, and I spent much time trying to see what they were forever complaining about. There always seemed to be some catastrophe impending up in that sky parlor, but it never appeared to reach a climax.

Charming to watch is the bluebird nestling; cheery and gentle like the parents, he seems to escape the period of helplessness that many birds suffer from, perhaps because he is patient enough to stay in the nest till his wings are ready to use. The mocking-bird baby has a far different time. Victim of a devouring ambition that will not let him rest till either legs or wings will bear him, he scrambles out upon his native tree, stretches, plumes a little in a jerky, hurried way, and then boldly launches out in the air—alas!—to come flop to the ground, where he is an easy prey to boys and cats, both of whom are particularly fond of young mocking-birds. These parents are wiser than the crow blackbirds, for not a sound betrays the accident in the family, unless, indeed, the little one is disturbed, when they make noise enough. They keep out of sight, no doubt closely watching the straggler until he gets away from people, for although he has proved that he cannot fly, the young mocker is by no means discouraged; he trusts to his legs, and usually at once starts off on a run "anywhere, anywhere, out (in) the world." When far enough away for them to feel safe in doing so, the parents come down and feed and comfort the wanderer, and it is a day or two before his wings are of much use to him.

The most imperious young bird I know is the robin. He is perfectly sure he has a right to attention, and he intends to have it. If he is neglected too long and gets hungry, he calls loudly and impatiently, jerking himself up with a ludicrous air of stamping his feet. Even when he does condescend to go to the lawn with mamma, it is not to seek his food—far from it! It is to follow her around, and call every moment or two for something to eat. The idea that his individual exertions have anything to do with the food supply seems never to occur to him. He expects the fat morsels to fall into his mouth as they always have, and why should they not? He will soon be taught, for even baby-birds have to be educated.

We have assumed in our easy-going way that birds "toil not" because they "do not spin," because they have not surrounded themselves with a thousand artificial wants, as we have. But the truth is that nobody can work harder than a pair of robins, for example, with four or five hungry mouths to fill, and every mouthful to be hunted up as it is wanted. No one would guess what an ever-yawning cavern a baby robin's mouth is, till he has tried to bring up a nestling himself. I once kept two small boys busy several days at high wages, digging worms for one young bird, and then I believe he starved to death.

The training of our winged neighbors is most interesting, but so cautiously carried on that we rarely see it, though we may often hear the robin, oriole, whip-poor-will, and many others receive instruction in singing. I have once or twice surprised young birds at their lessons, as for instance, a pewee family learning to hover over the daisies, a beautiful operation of their parents which I never tired of watching. I was behind a blind when they came, a little flock of five or six. They were very playful, and kept near together, flying low over the grass, alighting in a row on the edge of a pail, coming up on the clothes-line, banging awkwardly against the house, and in every way showing ignorance and youth. I studied one for a long time as he balanced himself on the clothes-line and looked off at the antics of his brothers trying to learn the hovering. One of the parents flew out over the tall flowers, poising himself gracefully, his body held perfectly erect, legs half drawn up, turning his head this way and that, hanging thus in the air several seconds in one spot, then suddenly darting off to another like a humming-bird. The little ones in a row close together on a low branch of a shrub, looked on, and in a moment two or three sallied out and tried the same movement. They could fly well enough, but when they tried to pause on wing the failure was disastrous. Some tumbled out of sight into the daisies, others recovered themselves with violent efforts and returned hastily to the perch, complaining loudly. Then the parents brought food, and this went on for some time, while all the time the air was full of gentle twitters and calls, much baby-talk, and a little parental instruction no doubt.

A delightful field of work awaits the young naturalist of to-day. Our predecessors have devoted their energies to classifying and arranging. They have dissected and weighed and measured every part of the little bodies; they know to a fraction the length of wings and tails; they have pulled to pieces the nests, "clutched" the eggs, and blown and mounted and labeled and set up in cases the whole external of the little creatures. All that can be learned by violence, all the characteristics evolved by fear and distress are duly set down in the books. You shall find a catalogue of the robin's possessions in the shape of feathers and bones, pictures of his internal anatomy, illustrations of his work in nest building, and specimens in all stages, but in the whole world of these books you shall not find the robin. The soul of the robin has escaped them, it is not to be taken by force.

I do not find fault; it needed to be done, but happily—let us hope—it is done, and a more enticing field is now open, namely: to make personal acquaintance with the birds, find out how they live, their manners and customs, and their individual characters. This is one of the most charming studies in the world, but much more is required than a gun and a little or much scientific knowledge. There is infinite patience, perseverance, untiring devotion, and more,—a quick eye and ear, and a sympathetic heart. If you do not love the birds you cannot understand them.

This is the pleasant path opening now, and in some ways it is particularly suited to woman with her great patience and quiet manners. Once interested in the lives in the "upper stories," you will find them most absorbing; novels will pall upon you, fancy work seem frivolous, society duties a bore, and talk—loud enough to interfere with listening—an impertinence.

BIRD-STUDY IN A SOUTHERN STATE.

He loved the ever deepening brown
Of summer twilights on the enchanted hills;
Where he might listen to the starts and thrills
Of birds that sang and rustled in the trees,
Or watch the footsteps of the wandering breeze,
And the bird's shadows as they fluttered by,
Or slowly wheeled across the unclouded sky.
Richard Watson Gilder.

II.

BIRD-STUDY IN A SOUTHERN STATE.

The most interesting experience in several years of bird-study was a trip to a Southern State for the purpose of making acquaintance with the mocking-bird.

Adventures began before the lights of New York sank below the horizon; adventures more strange than agreeable, for the journey was by steamer. Hardly had we passed out of the bay when there began a gentle roll which speedily sent passengers to bed. When we passed Long Branch the motion was a steady rock from side to side, that made one feel like a baby in a cradle, and before bedtime it was a violent swing that flung one about like a toy, and tossed the furniture around like doll-house belongings.

Holding on to the side of the berth with both hands, I passed the night listening to the labored strokes of the engine and the crashing of the loosened freight in the hold, and entertained by the eccentric conduct of the loose articles in my state-room, a trunk, chair, life-preserver, plate, saucer, and teaspoon, which with one accord, and in spite of all I could do by most ingenious wedging, joined in a peculiar dance between the outer wall and the inner partition of my room. At one moment they rested quietly in their several ways, against the wall; the steamer lurched, and all started madly across the floor, the heavy things first, and the lighter bringing up the rear, each banging violently against the partition, with thump, rattle, or jingle according to its nature, then in a moment dashing back so furiously that I feared to see the thin planks yield and my trunk go out to sea by itself. Not that I cared for my trunk—my life was the subject that interested me at the time. Outside, too, the doors and blinds rattled, the tiller-chain chattered and wailed and sobbed like a woman in distress, and above all other sounds rose the dismal fog horn, for a pall of mist had settled over us.

Day differed from night only in being light, for the sole prospect from the guards was one moment the fog above, where the sky should be, the next the depths of the sea yawning as if to receive the ship into its bosom. In this manner, during two days and three nights, we rolled on to our destination, and for days after my feet touched blessed Mother Earth I reeled and staggered like a drunken man.

After the storm, the calm. There followed upon this rough voyage weeks of quiet, delightful bird-study, whose long sunny-days were passed in the fragrant depths of pine groves, under arching forest of sweet-gum trees, or on the shore of the salt marsh; but wherever, or however, always following and spying out the ways of the feathered world.

The bird of the South—the mocking-bird, was the first object of study. By day he was watched and noted, during the long twilight he was listened to, and at midnight sleep was often banished by his wonderful and enchanting voice. Gray and inconspicuous in coloring, we all know him in the cage; but how different in freedom! how wild and bewitching his song! how wise and knowing his ways! how well worth weeks of study is this one bird!

Here were dozens of other birds also. What keen delight to one fresh from the town, to look over the marsh where

10

"Leagues and leagues of marsh grass, waist high, broad in the blade,
Green and all of a height, and unflecked with a light or a shade,
Stretch leisurely off in a pleasant plain
To the terminal blue of the main;"

to watch the great snowy heron sweeping over with broad white wing, tripping gracefully about on the edges of the channels, and toward night betaking itself to a line of trees in the distance, that looked as if full of snowy blossoms that moved and changed about and at last settled for the night; to see the bald eagle catch a big fish and call his mate to help him eat it; to watch the lesser tern hover with yellow bill pointed downward and sharp eye fixed on the water, and at length stiffen his wings and dive head first into it, bringing out his prey, and filling the air with cries in a complaining, squealing tone that always reminds one of a young pig; to gaze fascinated at the bewitching flight of the ring-plover, sweeping low over the water in a small flock, now almost invisible as the sombre-colored backs turn toward you, now suddenly flashing bright as silver when the breasts come into sight, moving in perfect unison as if impelled by one will. More, many more birds of the marsh attract and draw one, but inland is the mocking-bird, and after a walk along the shore, always my feet turned to the groves and the fields where the matchless bird lives his life.

To see, as well as hear a wild mocking-bird sing, is worth a journey, even over the rolling deep. I passed hours in a pleasant grove beyond the gardens and fields, watching and listening to one bird whose concert hall it was. The grove was the audience room where one might be in the shade and not too conspicuous in watching him. His chosen place was in the sunshine, for this bird is a sun-worshiper. I always found him singing when I reached the spot. Perhaps on the top spike of a young pine-tree, balanced on one, or sometimes on two adjoining top twigs—which of course stand straight up—stood the singer, madly shouting his most peculiar medley. He looked at me as I passed near his perch, but did not pause in his song. After I had taken my seat he flew—singing as he went—alighted nearer, on the upper sprig of a cedar, turned his eyes upon me, and treated me to another performance, while I looked and listened enchanted.

Nor was I the only listener. Ever and anon while absorbed in the entertainment, or waiting, breathless, for a new note, I was startled by a rustle, and a low "Good evenin' Missis," and glanced up to see a negro stealing along in a stealthy way. It might be a woman with a big bundle or basket on her head, possibly a slouching young man or "boy" with an air of interest in my eccentric proceedings, or a group of youngsters with nothing particular to do, but one and all perfectly silent in movement. No wonder they know all about the birds, and lay violent hands on eggs, nests, or nestlings as they choose, creeping around as they do without a sound. It is only surprising that a bird is left in the State, so persistently do they rob the nests. Naturally the mocking-bird, for which they can always find purchasers, is the most desirable, and white as well as black persecute that bird unceasingly.

"You can't keep them from the negroes," said a young white man. "I've often been watching a nest to get the young ones myself, but some nig was sure to take it before me."

Speaking of negroes, I never saw so many idle men and grown boys. Not a spot could be found so secluded that one or more did not soon make his appearance. Selecting the quiet yard of a summer cottage, a deserted-looking place not yet opened for the season, in which to study the ways of the birds in peace, I was often disturbed by a negro passing across the lawn, taking no heed of fences, for there's no sort of a fence in that country that they will not pass over as if it were not there. Of course this always put to flight the dramatis personæ of my study. One day an interesting (or interested) person of color appeared on the scene equipped for white-washing, and proceeded to adorn tree trunks, fences, buildings, etc., etc., relieving his labors by questioning me about northern manners and customs. On another occasion when I was looking anxiously to see a certain family of nestlings make exit from the nest, a building that I supposed to be a shut-up store-room was thrown open, a wash-tub appeared before the door, and I found that a family of eight, including four children, had moved in, not thirty feet from my chosen seat, and of course to the utter destruction of any seclusion.

I could not select a single spot in the neighborhood, favorable to quiet study, without having it made desolate or turned into a thoroughfare. The loveliest place I found at all was a footpath passing for about fifty feet through a fringe of low cedar, sweet gum trees, and shrubs loaded with pink lily-of-the-valley shaped blossoms. Across the path ran a brooklet, a mere thread of water, so shallow that small birds stood in the middle to bathe, though it deepened into a pool below, where frogs croaked and plunged. It was cool; it was quiet, far from the everywhere present negro hut; there was no sound but the trickle of the streamlet as it fell into the pool, and the softened roar of the ocean beyond the wide salt marsh.

To this nook I went every day, always trying to surprise the birds at their usual occupations, but never quite succeeding; for steal in quietly as I might I always heard low remarks, a slight flutter of wings, and usually saw a dark form or two departing near the ground behind some shrub. Slowly and quietly, however, I took my seat on a bank close under a thick bush,—while the silence around me was as profound as if no wing had ever fluttered there,—and became as motionless as circumstances would allow, for beside the birds there were other tenants not half so shy.

After a few moments, when the ripple I caused had died away, sounds of life began again; unknown water creatures made queer noises in the pool below, low bird tones, unfamiliar scraps of song fell on the ear, ordinary ways were resumed.

In this pleasant place I made acquaintance with the painted-finch, or nonpareil, who was least frightened of the small birds, and stood patiently on a cedar twig till I became quiet, then came down in plain sight, waded up to the tops of his firm little legs in the water, and deliberately took his bath before my very face. Here also I had a call from Bob White, who cautiously lifted a striped cap and a very bright eye above the grass tops to look at me. He did not introduce himself; indeed, after a moment's steady gaze his head dropped and I saw him no more, but I heard him rustle in the grass on the way to the strawberries, of which he demands—and gets—his share.

Ruin fell upon this charming retreat in this wise. One day on my approach I saw commotion in the shrubs and two negroes at work chopping great branches out on each side of the path, letting in the sun to my bank, and turning it into a hideous wreck. I protested.

"Why is this? What are you doing?"

"Oh, we're just cuttin' some pea-poles!" they replied calmly. They had been too lazy or too indifferent to step ten feet on one side into the thicker copse, and leave the pretty path in its beauty, and the mischief was done, and after all it was not my business. I passed on.

Bird-study has other annoyances in that part of the world beside the human beings of whom I have spoken. Next, perhaps, are the sufferings which wring the heart all the while. John Burroughs has written the tragedies of the nests; he could add a chapter more tragical than all, should he visit the haunts of the mocking-bird. Nothing can be more dreadful than the systematic and persistent war made upon this bird, of which nevertheless every Southerner is proud.

Lastly, the hindrances which Dame Nature herself throws around her mysteries. There are the prickly pears, sowed broadcast over the land so thickly that one can hardly avoid stepping on them, with thorns sharp as needles, and as long. One of an inch in length that I had the curiosity to examine had forty-five thorns, equal to two papers of number six sharps, that stuck out in every direction, and would pass through an ordinary shoe with perfect ease. This interesting vegetable has no local attachments whatever, and readily clings to any part of one's garment.

Then there are the mosquitoes with which the same careful mother peoples the groves, even in April, industrious little creatures not in the least enervated by the climate. But her grand dependence, judiciously settled indeed, is on the sand flies. Wherever there is not a howling gale—there are the flies in millions, most indefatigable and maddening of pests. And finally, to take home with you, to remind you pleasantly of her hospitalities when you have reached your own room, is the tick!

Ties from the outer world began at last to draw. The birdlings in the nest were not ready to come out, and growing impatient I drew upon the knowledge—or rather the ignorance—of the residents and heard some surprising statements, which further observation, however, did not confirm. That the mocking-bird baby lives for three weeks in the nest; that part of that time the parents carry the nestlings about on their backs; that when old enough the young are pushed out of their nest, and always fall to the ground.

And the authors of these fables were grown-up, and had passed their lives among the mocking-birds. I curbed my impatience, stayed another week, and saw all the nestlings out, and the nest deserted.

Another charge also fell to the ground on careful observation. The farmers complain—as farmers are apt to complain of their best friends, the birds—that the mocking-bird eats strawberries. I set myself to watch a fine patch full of ripe and tempting berries, several times when no one was near. Many birds came about, mocking-birds, crows, kingbirds, orchard orioles, and others. The mocking-birds ran down between the rows of vines catching grasshoppers, the crows did the same service, walking with dignity. The kingbirds chased flies, the orioles searched the fruit trees for insects. One and all were working in the interest of the strawberry grower. And while I watched, an hour or more at a time, not even for dessert after filling their stomachs with insects, did one take a berry, which I am sure they might be considered to have earned.

I know one lady—would there were more like her—who owns a garden on Long Island, and when her gardener comes in and says something *must* be done to prevent the birds destroying fruit, calmly says: "Certainly, set out another row of plants. Let us have enough for the birds by all means, and for ourselves too."

THE MOCKING-BIRD'S NEST.

Whate'er birds did or dreamed, this bird could say.
Then down he shot, bounced airily along
The sward, twitched in a grasshopper, made song
Midflight, perched, prinked, and to his art again.
Sweet Science, this large riddle read me plain:
How may the death of that dull insect be
The life of yon trim Shakespeare, on the tree?
Sidney Lanier.
III.
THE MOCKING-BIRD'S NEST.
"Superb and sole upon a plumèd spray
That o'er the general leafage boldly grew,"

as literally as though Lanier had sketched that particular bird, stood the first free mocking-bird I ever heard. His perch was the topmost twig of the tallest tree in the group. It was a cedar, perhaps fifteen feet high, around which a jasmine vine had clambered, and that morning opened a cluster of fragrant blossoms at his feet, as though an offering to the most noted singer on our side of the globe. As I drew near he turned his clear, bright eye upon me, and sang a welcome to North Carolina; and several hours later, when the moon rose high over the waters of the Sound, he completed his perfect performance with a serenade, the like of which I fear I may never hear again. I chose to consider his attentions personal, because, of all the household, I am sure I was the only one who listened, and I had passed over many miles of rolling and tossing ocean to make his acquaintance.

Nothing would have been easier, or more delightful, than to pitch one's tent in a certain pine grove not far away, and pass days and weeks in forgetting the world of cares, and reading favorite books, lulled at all hours of day and night by the softened roar of the ocean and the wonderful bird

"Singing the song of everything,

Consummate sweet, and calm."

But it was not merely as singer that I wished to know him; nor to watch his dainty and graceful ways as he went about the daily duties of food-hunting, singing, and driving off marauders, which occupied his hours from dawn to late evening, and left him spirit enough for many a midnight rhapsody. It was in his domestic relations that I desired to see him,—the wooing of the bride and building the nest, the training of mocking-bird babies and starting them in the world; and no loitering and dreaming in the pine grove, however tempting, would tell me this. I must follow him to his more secluded retreats, see where he had set up his homestead.

Thoreau—or is it Emerson?—says one always finds what he looks for, and of course I found my nests. One pair of birds I noticed through the courtship, the selection of the site, the building and occupying of the nest; another couple, already sitting when discovered, I watched through the incubation and nursing of the little ones, and at last assisted in giving them a fair chance for their lives and a start in the world. It may be thought that my assistance was not particularly valuable; the birds shared this opinion; none the less, but for my presence not one of those birdlings would be free and happy to-day, as I hope and believe they are. To the study of these two households I gave nearly every hour of daylight, in all weathers, for a month, and of the life that went on in and around them I can speak from personal knowledge; beyond that, and at other times in his life, I do not profess to know the mocking-bird.

The bird whose nest-making I witnessed was the one whose performance I chose to consider a welcome, and his home was in the pine grove, a group of about twenty trees, left from the original forest possibly, at any rate nearly a hundred feet high, with all branches near the top, as though they had grown in close woods. They were quite scattering now, and lower trees and shrubs flourished in their shade, making a charming spot, and a home worthy even of this superb songster. The bird himself was remarkably friendly. Seeming to appreciate my attitude of admiring listener, he often perched on the peak of a low roof (separated only by a carriage drive from the upper "gallery" where I sat), and sang for hours at a time, with occasional lunches; or, as Lanier, his most ardent lover, has it,—

"Then down he shot, bounced airily along

The sward, twitched in a grasshopper, made song

Midflight, perched, prinked, and to his art again."

Whatever he did, his eyes were upon me; he came to the corner nearest me to sing, and was so intelligent in look and bearing that I believe he liked a quiet listener.

His wooing, however, the bird did not intend me to see, though two or three times I surprised him at it. The first part that I chanced upon was curious and amusing. A female, probably the "beloved object," stood demurely on one of the dead top branches of a large tree down in the garden, while her admirer performed fantastic evolutions in the air about her. No flycatcher ever made half the eccentric movements this aerial acrobat indulged in. He flew straight up very high, executing various extraordinary turns and gyrations, so rapidly they could not be followed and described, and came back singing; in a moment he departed in another direction, and repeated the grotesque performance. He was plainly exerting himself to be agreeable and entertaining, in mocking-bird style, and I noticed that every time he returned from an excursion he perched a little nearer his audience of one, until, after some time, he stood upon the same twig, a few inches from her. They were facing and apparently trying to stare each other out of countenance; and as I waited, breathless, to see what would happen next, the damsel coquettishly flitted to another branch. Then the whole scene was repeated; the most singular and graceful evolutions, the songs, and the gradual approach. Sometimes, after alighting on a top twig, he dropped down through the branches, singing, in a way to suggest the "dropping song" so graphically described by Maurice Thompson, but never really falling, and never touching the ground. Each performance ended in his reaching the twig which she occupied and her flight to another, until at last, by some apparently mutual agreement, both flew, and I saw no more.

A remarkable "dance" which I also saw, with the same bird as principal actor, seems to me another phase of the wooing, though I must say it resembled a war-dance as well; but love is so like war among the lower orders, even of men, that it is hard to distinguish between them. I shall not try to decide, only to relate, and, I beg to say, without the smallest exaggeration. The dances I saw were strictly *pas-de-deux*, and they always began by a flash of wings and two birds alighting on the grass, about a foot apart. Both instantly drew themselves up perfectly erect, tail elevated at an angle of forty-five degrees, and wings held straight down at the sides. Then followed a most droll dance. Number one stood like a statue, while number two pranced around, with short, mincing steps and dainty little hops which did not advance him an inch; first he passed down the right, then turned and went down the left, all in the queer, unnatural manner of short hops and steps, and holding himself rigidly erect, while number one always faced the dancer, whichever way he turned. After a few moments of this movement, number one decided to participate, and when his partner moved to the right he did the same; to the left he still accompanied him, always facing, and maintaining the exact distance from him. Then number two described a circle around number one, who turned to face him with short hops where he stood. Next followed a *chassé* of both birds to the right; then a separation, one dancing to the right and the other to the left, always facing, and always slowly and with dignity. This stately minuet they kept up for some time, and appeared so much like a pair of old-fashioned human dancers that when, on one occasion, number two varied the performance by a spring over the head of his partner, I was startled, as if an old gentleman had suddenly hopped over the head of the grand dame his *vis-à-vis*. When this strange new figure was introduced, number one proved equal to the emergency, hopping backward, and turning so dexterously that when his partner alighted they were facing, and about a foot apart, as before. The object of all this was very uncertain to a looker-on. It might be the approaches of love, and quite as probably the wary beginnings of war, and the next feature of the programme was not explanatory; they rose together in the air ten feet or more, face to face, fluttering and snatching at each other, apparently trying to clinch; succeeding in doing so, they fell to the ground, separated just before they touched it, and flew away. O wings! most maddening to a bird-student.

It was not very long after these performances, which seem to me to belong to the courtship period, when I noticed that my bird had won his bride, and they were busy house-hunting. The place they apparently preferred, and at last fixed upon, was at an unusual height for mocking-birds, near the top of one of the tall pines, and I was no less surprised than pleased to see them lay the foundation of their home in that spot. I congratulated myself that at least one brood in North Carolina would have a chance to come to maturity and be free; and so persistent is the warfare waged against this bird—unfortunately marketable at any stage from the egg—that I almost doubt if another will. The day after they began building a northwest storm set in, and for three days we had high winds and cold weather. In spite of this, the brave birds persevered, and finished their nest during those three days, although much of the time they made infrequent trips. It was really most touching to watch them at their unnatural task, and remember that nothing but the cruelty of man forced them to it (one nest had been destroyed). Their difficulty was to get up against the wind, and, having little experience in flying upward, they made the natural mistake of starting from the foot of their chosen tree. Sometimes, at first, they flew with the body almost perpendicular; and afterwards, when they held the body in proper position, they wished to go so directly up that they turned the head back over the shoulder to see where they were going. The wind, too, beat them far out of their course, and they were obliged to alight and rest, occasionally being forced to cling to the trunk of a tree to recover breath and strength to go on. They never attempted to make the whole ascent at once, but always stopped four or five times, perching on the ends of fallen branches, of which there were eight or ten below the living part of the pine. Even when no wind disturbed them, they made these pauses on the way, and it was always a hard task to reach the top. They learned, after a few days, however, to begin their ascent at a distance, and not approach the tree till at least half as high as they wished to go, which simplified the matter very much. It was beautiful to see them, upon reaching the lowest of the living branches, bound gayly up, as though over a winding stair, to the particular spot they had fixed upon.

During the building I missed the daily music of the singer. Occasionally he alighted on the roof, looked over at me, and bubbled out a few notes, as much as to say, "You must excuse me now; I am very busy;" but all the time I hoped that while sitting was going on I should have him back. I reckoned ignorantly; I did not know my bird. No sooner was he the possessor of a house and family than he suddenly became very wary. No more solos on the roof; no more confidential remarks; no more familiarities of any sort. Now he must beware of human beings, and even when on the grass he held himself very erect, wings straight down, every instant on guard. His happiness demanded expression in song, certainly, but instead of confining himself to the roof he circled the lawn, which was between two and three hundred feet wide. If he began in a group of cedars on the right, he sang awhile there, then flew to the fence next the road without a pause in the music, and in a few minutes passed to the group of pines at the left, perched on a dead branch, and finished his song there. It was most tantalizing, though I could but admit it a proof of intelligence.

Another change appeared in the bird with the advent of family cares: he was more belligerent; he drove the bluebird off the lawn, he worried the tufted titmouse when it chanced to alight on his tree, and in the most offensive way claimed ownership of pine-trees, lawn, and all the fence bordering the same. Neighboring mocking-birds disputed his claim, and many a furious chase took place among the trees. (So universal is their habit of insisting upon exclusive right to certain grounds that two mocking-birds are never found nesting very near each other, in that part of the country. This I was assured, and found it true of those I observed.) These little episodes in his life kept the pine-tree bird from dullness, while his mate was engaged in the top of the tall pine, where, by the way, he went now and then to see how she was getting on. Sometimes his spouse received him amiably, but occasionally, I regret to say, I heard a "huff" from the nest that said plainly, "Don't you touch those eggs!" And what was amusing, he acknowledged her right to dictate in the matter, and meekly took his departure. Whenever she came down for a lunch, he saw her instantly, and was ready for a frolic. He dropped to the grass near her, and they usually indulged in a lively romp, chasing each other over and through the trees, across the yard, around the garden, and back to the lawn, where she went on with her eating, and he resumed his singing.

While I was watching the pine-tree household, the other nest, in the top of a low, flat-topped cedar, perhaps twenty-five feet high, and profusely fringed with Spanish moss, became of even more interest. I could not see into the nest, for there was no building high enough to overlook it, but I could see the bird when he stood upon the edge. Sitting, in a warm climate, is not particularly close work. Although the weather was cool, yet when the sun was out the sitter left her nest from six to eight minutes at a time, and as often as once in twenty minutes. Of course in rain she had not so much liberty, and on some days left only when her mate was ready to take her place, which he frequently did.

On the ninth day of my watching (I had not seen the beginning of the sitting), the 3d of May, I found work was over and the youngsters were out. There was much excitement in the cedar-tree, but in a quiet way; in fact, the birds became so silent and so wary in approaching the nest that it required the closest watching to see them go or come, and only occasionally could I detect any food in the beak. I discovered very soon that mocking-bird babies are brought up on hygienic principles, and have their meals with great regularity. For some time both parents were exceedingly busy, going and coming almost constantly; then there came a rest of a half hour or more, during which no food was brought. Each bird had its own way of coming to the tree. Madam came over the roof of the cottage where I sat, and was exposed to view for only a few feet, over which she passed so quickly and silently that I had to be constantly on the alert to see her at all. The singer had another way, and by rising behind a hickory-tree beyond the cedar managed to keep a screen of branches between him and myself nearly every foot of the way. I could see them both almost every time, but I could not always tell whether they carried food. Now the bluebird, honest soul, always stops in plain sight to rest, with his mouth full of dainties for his young brood, and a robin will stand staring at one for two minutes with three or four wriggling worms in his beak. It is quite a different affair in the mocking-bird family, as is certainly natural, after the persecution it has endured. No special fear of me was the cause,—it is a marked peculiarity of the bird; and I think, with a little study, one could learn to know exactly the moment the eggs hatch by the sudden silence and wariness of both birds. Poor little creatures! a sympathetic friend hates to add to the anxiety they suffer, and he cannot help a feeling of reproach when the brave little head of the family alights on the fence, and looks him straight in the eye, as if to demand why he is subjected to all this annoyance. I had to console myself by thinking that I was undoubtedly a providence to him; for I am certain that nothing but my watching him so conspicuously that every negro within a mile saw me, saved his family to him, so low and easy of access was the nest.

The day those nestlings were one week old they uttered their first cry. It was not at all a "peep," but a cry, continued a few seconds; at first only when food was offered to them, but as they increased in age and strength more frequently. It was much like a high-pitched " - - ," and on the first day there was but one voice, which grew rapidly stronger as the hours went by. The next day another and a weaker cry joined the first, now grown assured and strong. But the music of the father was hushed the moment the youngsters began; from that time until they had left the nest, he sang not a note in my hearing. Perhaps he was too busy, though he never seemed to work so hard as the robin or oriole; but I think it was cautiousness, for the trouble of those parents was painful to witness. They introduced a new sound among their musical notes, a harsh squawk; neither dog nor negro could cross the yard without being saluted with it. As for me, though I was meekness itself, taking the most obscure position I could find, and remaining as absolutely motionless as possible, they eyed me with suspicion; from the first they "huffed" at me, and at this point began to squawk the moment I entered the gate. On one occasion I discovered that by changing my seat I could actually see the nest, which I much desired; so I removed while the birds were absent. Madam was the first to return, with a beakful of food; she saw me instantly, and was too much excited to dispose of her load. She came to my side of her tree, squawked loudly, flapping her wings and jerking herself about. I remained motionless and did not look at her, pretending to be absorbed in my book; but she refused to be mollified. It evidently did not please her to have me see so plainly; she desired to retain the friendly screen of leaves which had secured her a small measure of privacy. I could not blame her; I felt myself intrusive; and at last I respected her wishes and returned to my old place, when she immediately calmed down and administered the food she had held till then. Poor mother! those were trying times. Her solicitude overpowered her discretion, and her manner proclaimed to every one within hearing that the nestlings were out. Then, too, on the eighth day the little ones added their voices, and soon called loudly enough to attract the dullest of nest-robbers. I was so fearful lest that nest should be disturbed that I scarcely dared to sleep o' nights; the birds themselves were hardly more anxious than I was.

The eleventh day of the birdlings' life was exceedingly warm, without a breath of air stirring, suffocating to humanity, but preëminently inspiring to mocking-birds, and every singer within a mile of me, I am sure, was singing madly, excepting the newly made parent. Upon reaching my usual seat I knew at once, by the louder cry, that a young bird was out of the nest, and after some searching through the tree I found him,—a yellowish-drab little fellow, with very decided wing-markings, a tail perhaps an inch in length, and soft slate-colored spots, so long as almost to be streaks, on the breast. He was scrambling about the branches, always trying to get a higher place, calling and perking his insignificant tail in true mocking-bird fashion. I think the parents disapproved this early ambition, for they did not feed him for a long time, though they passed him to go to the nest. So far from being lightened, their cares were greatly increased by the precociousness of the youngster, and from this moment their trouble and worry were grievous to see. So much self-reliance has the mocking-bird, even in the nest, that he cannot be kept there until his legs are strong enough to bear his weight, or his wings ready to fly. The full-grown spirit of the race blossoms out in the young one at eleven days, and for several more he is exposed to so many dangers that I wonder there is one left in the State.

The parents, one after the other, came down on to a bush near my seat to remonstrate with me; and I must admit that so great was my sympathy, and so uncomfortable did I feel at adding in the least to their anxiety, that I should never have seen that young family fledged, only that I knew perfectly well what they did not, that I was a protection to them. I tried to reassure the mother by addressing her in her own language (as it were), and she turned quickly, looked, listened, and returned to her tree, quieted. This sound is a low whistling through the teeth, which readily soothes cage birds. It interests and calms them, though I have no notion what it means to them, for I am speaking an unknown tongue.

The baby on the tree was not quiet, climbing about the branches every moment that he was not engaged in dressing his feathers, the first and most important business of the newly emancipated nestling. After an hour or more of watching there was a sudden stir in the family, and the youngster made his appearance on the ground. He was not under the side of the tree on which he had been resting, so, although I did not see the passage, I knew he had not fallen, as he is popularly said to do, but flown as well as he was able. I started slowly down the yard to examine the little stranger, but was absolutely startled by a cry from the mother, that sounded exactly like "Go 'way!" as I have often heard a negro girl say it. Later it was very familiar, a yearning, anxious heart-aching sound to hear.

The youth was very lively, starting off at once on his travels, never for an instant doubting his own powers. I saw his first movement, which was a hop, and, what surprised and delighted me, accompanied by a peculiar lifting of the wings, of which I shall have more to say. He quickly hopped through the thin grass till he reached a fence, passed down beside it till a break in the pickets left an open place on the bottom board, sprang without hesitation upon that, and after a moment's survey of the country beyond dropped down on the farther side. Now that was a lane much frequented by negroes, and, being alarmed for his safety, I sent a boy after him, and in a moment had him in my hand. He was a beautiful little creature, having a head covered with downy dark feathers, and soft black eyes, which regarded me with interest, but not at all with fear. All this time, of course, the parents were scolding and crying, and I held him only long enough to look carefully at him, when I replaced him on the grass. Off he started at once, directly west,—like the "march of empire,"—went through the same fence again, but further down, and, as I could tell by the conduct of the parents, in a few moments was safely through a second fence into a comparatively retired old garden beyond, where I hoped he would be unmolested. Thus departed number one, with energy and curiosity, to investigate a brand-new world, fearless in his ignorance and self-confidence, although his entrance into the world had not been the triumphant fly we might look for, but an ignominious "flop," and was irresistibly and ludicrously suggestive of the manner of exit from the home nest of sundry individuals of our own race, which we consider of much greater importance.

The young traveler set out at exactly ten o'clock. As soon as he was out of sight, though not out of hearing,—for the youngster as well as the parents kept the whole world of boys and cats well informed of his whereabouts for three days,—I returned and gave my attention to number two, who was now out upon the native tree. This one was much more quiet than his predecessor. He did not cry, but occasionally uttered a mocking-bird squawk, though spending most of his time dressing his plumage, in preparation for the grand *entrée*. At twelve o'clock he made the plunge and came to the ground in a heap. This was plainly a bird of different disposition from number one; his first journey evidently tired him. He found the world hard and disappointing, so he simply stayed where he dropped in the middle of the path, and refused to move, though I touched him as a gentle reminder of the duty he owed to his parents and his family. He sat crouched upon the gravel and looked at me with calm black eye, showing no fear and certainly no intention of moving, even indulging in a nap while I waited.

Now appeared upon the scene several persons, both white and black, each of whom wanted a young mocking-bird for a cage; but I stood over him like a god-parent and refused to let any one touch him. I began to fear that I should have him on my hands at last, for even the parents seemed to appreciate his characteristics and to know that he could not be hurried, and both were still busy following the vagaries of number one. The mother now and then returned to

21

look after him and was greatly disturbed by his unnatural conduct—and so was I. He appeared stupid, as if he had come out too soon, and did not even know how to hop. It was twenty minutes by the watch before he moved. His mother's calls at last aroused him; he raised himself upon his shaky little legs, cried out, and started off exactly as number one had done,—westward, hopping, and lifting his wings at every step. Then I saw by the enormous amount of white on his wings that he was a singer. He went as far as the fence, and there he paused again. In vain did the mother come and scold; in vain did I try to push him along. He simply knew his own will, and meant to have it; the world might be strange, but he was not in the least interested. He rested in that spot fifteen or twenty minutes more, while I stood guard as before, and preserved him from cages of both negroes and whites. At last he did manage to squeeze through the fence, and, much relieved, I left him to the old birds, one of whom was down in the lot beyond the garden, no doubt following up his ambitious first-born.

Whoever, meanwhile, was left in the nest had a poor chance of food, and one was already crying. It was not until six o'clock that the birds seemed to remember the nestling; then it was well fed, and left again. Nothing would be easier than to follow the wandering youngsters, see how they got on and how soon they were able to fly, but this so disturbed the parents I had not the heart to do it; and besides I feared they would starve the infants, for one was never fed while I was near. Doubtless their experience of the human race forbade their confiding in the kindly intentions of any one. It was well that only two of the young appeared in one day, for keeping track of them was so serious a matter that two parents could scarcely manage it.

Number three differed from both of his elders; he was a cry-baby. He was not bright and lively like number one, and he did not squawk like number two, but he cried constantly, and at six P. M. I left him calling and crying at the top of his voice. Very early the next morning I hastened to the scene of yesterday's excitement. Number three was out on the tree. I could hear number two still crying and squawking in the garden, and from the position and labors of the male I concluded that number one was in the next lot. It was a dismal, damp morning, every grass-blade loaded with water, and a heavy fog driving in from the sea. I hoped number three would know enough to stay at home, but his fate was upon him, and no rain was ever wet enough to overcome destiny. At about eight o'clock he stretched his little wings and flew to the ground,—a very good flight for his family, nearly thirty feet, twice as far as either of his predecessors had gone; silently, too,—no fuss about it. He began at once the baby mocker's hop with lifted wings, headed for the west fence, jumped upon the lower board, squeezed through and was off down the garden before the usual crowd of spectators had collected to strive for his head. I was delighted. The parents, who were not near when he flew, came back soon and found him at once. I left him to them and returned to my place.

But silence seemed to have fallen upon the cedar, late so full of life. In vain I listened for another cry; in vain I watched for another visit from the parents. All were busy in the garden and lot, and if any baby were in that nest it must surely starve. Occasionally a bird came back, hunted a little over the old ground in the yard, perched a moment on the fence, and saluted me with a low squawk, but their interest in the place was plainly over.

After two hours I concluded the nest was empty; and a curious performance of the head of the late family convinced me it was so. He came quite near to me, perched on a bush in the yard, fixed his eyes on me, and then, with great deliberation, first huffed, then squawked, then sang a little, then flew. I do not know what the bird meant to say, but this is what it expressed to me: "You've worried us all through this trying time, but you didn't get one of our babies! Hurrah!"

In the afternoon I had the nest brought down to me. For foundation it had a mass of small twigs from six to eight inches long, crooked and forked and straight, which were so slightly held together that they could only be handled by lifting with both hands, and placing at once in a cloth, where they were carefully tied in. Within this mass of twigs was the nest proper, thick and roughly constructed, three and a half inches in inside diameter, made of string, rags, newspaper, cotton wadding, bark, Spanish moss, and feathers, lined with fine root fibre, I think. The feathers were not inside for lining, but outside on the upper edge. It was, like the foundation, so frail that, though carefully managed, it could only be kept in shape by a string around it, even after the mass of twigs had been removed. I have a last year's nest, made of exactly the same materials, but in a much more substantial manner; so perhaps the cedar-tree birds were not so skillful builders as some of their family.

The mocking-bird's movements, excepting in flight, are the perfection of grace; not even the cat-bird can rival him in airy lightness, in easy elegance of motion. In alighting on a fence, he does not merely come down upon it; his manner is fairly poetical. He flies a little too high, drops like a feather, touches the perch lightly with his feet, balances and tosses upward his tail, often quickly running over the tips of half a dozen pickets before he rests. Passing across the yard, he turns not to avoid a taller tree or shrub, nor does he go through it; he simply bounds over, almost touching it, as if for pure sport. In the matter of bounds the mocker is without a peer. The upward spring while singing is an ecstatic action that must be seen to be appreciated; he rises into the air as though too happy to remain on earth, and opening his wings, floats down, singing all the while. It is indescribable, but enchanting to see. In courtship, too, as related, he makes effective use of this exquisite movement. In simple food-hunting on the ground,—a most prosaic occupation, truly,—on approaching a hummock of grass he bounds over it instead of going around. In alighting on a tree he does not pounce upon the twig he has selected, but upon a lower one, and passes quickly up through the branches, as lithe as a serpent. So fond is he of this exercise that one which I watched amused himself half an hour at a time in a pile of brush; starting from the ground, slipping easily through up to the top, standing there a moment, then flying back and repeating the performance. Should the goal of his journey be a fence picket, he alights on the beam which supports it, and hops gracefully to the top.

Like the robin, the mocking-bird seeks his food from the earth, sometimes digging it, but oftener picking it up. His manner on the ground is much like the robin's; he lowers the head, runs a few steps rapidly, then erects himself very straight for a moment. But he adds to this familiar performance a peculiar and beautiful movement, the object of which I have been unable to discover. At the end of a run he lifts his wings, opening them wide, displaying their whole breadth, which makes him look like a gigantic butterfly, then instantly lowers his head and runs again, generally picking up something as he stops. A correspondent in South Carolina, familiar with the ways of the bird, suggests that his object is to startle the grasshoppers, or, as he expresses it, to "flush his game." I watched very closely and could not fix upon any theory more plausible, though it seemed to be weakened by the fact that the nestlings, as mentioned above, did the same thing before they thought of looking for food. The custom is not invariable; sometimes it is done, and sometimes not.

The mocking-bird cannot be said to possess a gentle disposition, especially during the time of nesting. He does not seem malicious, but rather mischievous, and his actions resemble the naughty though not wicked pranks of an active child. At that time he does, it must be admitted, lay claim to a rather large territory, considering his size, and enforces his rights with many a hot chase and noisy dispute, as remarked above. Any mocking-bird who dares to flirt a feather over the border of the ground he chooses to consider his own has to battle with him. A quarrel is a curious operation, usually a chase, and the war-cry is so peculiar and apparently so incongruous that it is fairly laughable. It is a rough breathing, like the "huff" of an angry cat, and a serious dispute between the birds reminds one of nothing but a disagreement in the feline family. If the stranger does not take the hint, and retire at the first huff, he is chased, over and under trees and through branches, so violently that leaves rustle and twigs are thrust aside, as long as the patience or wind holds out. On one occasion the defender of his homestead kept up a lively singing all through the furious flight, which lasted six or eight minutes,—a remarkable thing.

To others than his own kind the mocker seems usually indifferent, with the single exception of the crow. So long as this bird kept over the salt marsh, or flew quite high, or even held his mouth shut, he was not noticed; but let him fly low over the lawn, and above all let him "caw," and the hot-headed owner of the place was upon him. He did not seem to have any special plan of attack, like the kingbird or the oriole; his aim appeared to be merely to worry the enemy, and in this he was untiring, flying madly and without pause around a perching crow until he took flight, and then attempting to rise above him. In this he was not always successful, not being particularly expert on the wing, though I have two or three times seen the smaller bird actually rest on the back of the foe for three or four seconds at a time.

The song of the free mocking-bird! With it ringing in my ear at this moment, after having feasted upon it and gloried in it day and night for many weeks, how can I criticise it! How can I do otherwise than fall into rhapsody, as does almost every one who knows it and delights in it, as I do! It is something for which one might pine and long, as the Switzer for the Ranz-des-Vaches, and the more one hears it the more he loves it. I think there will never come a May in my life when I shall not long to fold my tent and take up my abode in the home of the mocking-bird, and yet I cannot say what many do. For variety, glibness, and execution the song is marvelous. It is a brilliant, bewildering exhibition, and one listens in a sort of ecstasy almost equal to the bird's own, for this, it seems to me, is the secret of the power of his music; he so enjoys it himself, he throws his whole soul into it, and he is so magnetic that he charms a listener into belief that nothing can be like it. His manner also lends enchantment; he is seldom still. If he begins in a cedar-tree, he soon flies to the fence, singing as he goes, thence takes his way to a roof, and so on, changing his place every few minutes, but never losing a note. His favorite perch is the top spire of a pointed tree, low cedar or young pine, where he can bound into the air as already described, spread his wings, and float down, never omitting a quaver. It seems like pure ecstasy; and however critical one may be, he cannot help feeling deep sympathy with the joyous soul that thus expresses itself. With all the wonderful power and variety, the bewitching charm, there is not the "feeling," the heavenly melody, of the wood-thrush. As an imitator, I think he is much overrated. I cannot agree with Lanier that

"Whate'er birds did or dreamed, this bird could say;"

and that the birds are jealous of his song, as Wilson says, seems absurd. On the contrary, I do not think they recognize the counterfeit. The tufted titmouse called as loudly and constantly all day as though no mocking-bird shouted his peculiar and easily imitated call from the house-top; the cardinal grosbeak sang every day in the grove, though the mocker copied him more closely than any other bird. He repeats the notes, rattles out the call, but he cannot put the cardinal's soul into them. The song of every bird seems to me the expression of himself; it is a perfect whole of its kind, given with proper inflections and pauses, and never hurried; whereas, when the mocker delivers it, it is simply one more note added to his repertory, uttered in his rapid staccato, in his loud, clear voice, interpolated between incongruous sounds, without expression, and lacking in every way the beauty and attraction of the original.

The song consists entirely of short staccato phrases, each phrase repeated several times, perhaps twice, possibly five or six times. If he has a list of twenty or thirty,—and I think he has more,—he can make almost unlimited changes and variety, and can sing for two hours or longer, holding his listener spellbound and almost without consciousness that he has repeated anything.

So winning and so lasting is the charm with which this bird enthralls his lovers that scarcely had I left his enchanted neighborhood before everything else was forgotten, and there remain of that idyllic month only beautiful pictures and delightful memories.

"O thou heavenly bird!"

A TRICKSY SPIRIT.

Bright drops of tune, from oceans infinite
Of melody, sipped off the thin-edged wave
And trickling down the bank, discourses brave
Of serious matter that no man may guess,
Good-fellow greetings, cries of light distress;
All these but now within the house are heard:
O Death, wast thou too deaf to hear the bird?
Sidney Lanier.

IV.

A TRICKSY SPIRIT.

For bird-lovers who know the mocking-bird only as a captive in our houses he has few attractions: a mere loud-voiced echo of the inharmonious sounds man gathers about his home,—car-bells, street cries, and other unpleasing noises,—and choosing for his performances the hours one wants to sleep. Unfortunate is the neighborhood in which one is kept. Such was my feeling about the bird before I knew him in freedom, where he has a song of his own. But in my search for native birds I often saw the mocker, was surprised to notice his intelligence of look and manner, and at last took one into my bird-room, resolving that the moment he began to "mock" he should be given to some one who liked having the street in his house. My bird was very obliging in the matter; six months I watched him daily, and he was kind enough not to utter a sound, except an occasional harsh "chack." Probably he had too much liberty and too many interests about him; whatever the reason, I thanked him for it, and heartily enjoyed the study of his manners.

The bird was perhaps the most intelligent one I ever watched, the cat-bird being his only rival in that regard. Fear was unknown to him, and from the moment of his arrival he was interested in everything that took place around him; looking at each bird in succession; making close study of every member of the family; noticing the sounds of the street, including the sparrow broils on the porch-roof; in fact, extremely wide-awake and observing. To the goldfinch's song he gave attention, standing motionless except for a slight nervous jerk of one wing, looking and listening as intently as though studying the notes for future use. The freedom of the birds in the room surprised him, as he showed plainly by the eager glances with which he followed every movement and marked each act. Upon joining the party of the free, he took note of pictures in a newspaper, distinguishing objects in the cut, which he tried to pick up, as a small wheel and a bar. In colors he had a choice, and his selection was red; from a vase of roses of many hues he never failed to draw out the red one to pull it to pieces on the floor.

Liberty the mocking-bird emphatically enjoyed, and at once recognized a string attached to his door as a device to deprive him of it; after vainly trying to pick it apart, he betook himself to another cage, and refused to go back to his own. In any strange cage he stood quietly while I walked up to him, and made no attempt to leave his quarters, knowing perfectly well that I did not care to shut the door upon him; but when at home I could not lift my hands, or make the slightest movement, without causing him to dart out of the cage instantly. Having contention with his room-mates about the bits of apple put out for all to enjoy, he often carried away a piece to eat at his leisure. From habit he flew first to the top of a cage, that being his favorite perching place; but he evidently appreciated that, if he dropped the morsel, he should lose it through the wires; and after looking one side and the other, plainly satisfying himself of this fact, he went to the table with it. I never before saw a bird who did not have to learn the treacherous nature of cage roofs by experience. He appeared to work things out in his mind,—to reason, in truth. One cold morning in spring, when the furnace fire was out, a large, brilliant lamp was put by his cage to take off the chill, for he felt changes keenly. He seemed to understand it at once, and though, no doubt, it was his first experience of warmth from a light, he drew as near it as possible, and remained there perfectly quiet until the sun warmed the room and it was removed. Fear, as I said, he knew not, coming freely upon the desk, or even upon my lap, after apple or bread, or anything he fancied.

It was plain to see that this bird's first week with us was one of quiet study and observation. Not a movement of bird or man escaped his notice. He wished to understand, to take measure of his neighbors, to be master of the situation. This was manifested not only by his thoughtful manner and his wise and knowing looks, but by his subsequent conduct. During this period, also, he submitted to impositions from all the birds, even the smallest, without resentment. The wood-thrush easily drove him away from the apple; the little goldfinch chased him from his perch. He appeared to be meekness itself; but he was biding his time, he was making up his mind.

The first time the mocking-bird's door was opened he was not in the least surprised; no doubt, seeing others at liberty, he had expected it. At any rate, whatever his emotions, he instantly ran out on the perch placed in his doorway and surveyed his new world from this position. He was in no panic, not even in haste. When fully ready, he began his tour of inspection. First, to see if he really could reach the trees without, through those large, clear openings, he tried the windows, each of the three, but gently, not bouncing against them so violently as to fall to the floor, as more impetuous or less intelligent birds invariably do. Having proved each to be impassable, he was satisfied, and never tried again. Next, the ceiling interested him, and he flew all around the room, touching it gently everywhere, to assure himself of its nature. Convinced thus in a short time that his bounds were only widened, not removed, he went on to investigate closely what he had looked at from a distance; every bird-cage, inside as well as outside, if the owner happened to be away, every piece of furniture, pictures, books, and the pin-cushion,—where he was detained some time trying to carry off the large black heads of shawl-pins. The looking-glass absorbed him most completely on the first day; he flew against it, he hovered before it, slowly passing from bottom to top, alighted on top and looked over behind. I think he never solved that mystery to his own satisfaction, as he did that of the window-glass, which must have been quite as inexplicable, and it was never without a certain charm for him. He had no trouble in finding his way home: standing on a cage next to his, he saw his own door-perch, recognized it instantly (though he had been upon it only once), and, being hungry, dropped to it and ran into the cage.

The new-comer soon made thorough acquaintance with all his surroundings, and had leisure to turn his attention to a little matter yet unsettled; namely, his position in the small colony about him. The first few days, as already noted, he submitted to impositions; allowed himself to be driven away from the slices of apple on the matting, and turned from the bathing-dish on the floor. This was, however, the calm before the storm; though after all that is hardly a correct comparison, since there was never the least "storm" about his manner; he was composure itself. Having calmly and patiently considered the state of affairs, he suddenly asserted himself and took the position he felt was his right,—at the head. It soon became evident that he was prepared to defend the situation by force of arms. He conducted his conquests systematically, and subdued one after the other, beginning with the least.

The English goldfinch had been very saucy, scolding and flying over him as he went around the room, in the small bird's way; but one day it came to a sudden end. The goldfinch in his cage scolded the stranger for alighting too near his door. The mocking-bird turned, looked sharply at him, ruffled up his feathers, and jumped heavily to the top of the cage, turning one eye down upon his small foe with an air that said, "Who is this midget that insults me?" The finch was surprised, but did not fully appreciate the significance of this change of manner until he was let out, when he found at once that his amiable neighbor had suddenly become an active enemy, who chased him around the room till he panted for breath, and would not allow him a moment's rest or peace anywhere. This was strange experience for the little fellow, for heretofore none of the large birds had ever disturbed him. He scolded furiously, but he went; no one could stand against that determined approach. If the goldfinch wished to bathe, his persecutor took his place on the nearest perch, not a foot away, thus driving him to the floor with the intention of using the big birds' bath. He circled around the edge, but it did not suit, and he returned to his own, looked at his enemy, spattered a little, went back to the big dish, returned again, and thus vibrated between the two for several minutes, while the mocking-bird stood motionless, not offering any molestation, but plainly wishing to worry him. The final act occurred when both chanced accidentally to be in the same cage, not the home of either. The mocking-bird, without provocation, dropped from the upper perch upon the finch, who uttered a sharp cry and darted away. Two or three little feathers flew, though no hurt could be seen; but the smaller bird panted violently for a half hour, as though frightened, and for four or five hours sat quietly on a perch, neither eating nor making a sound,—a very unusual proceeding for the lively chattering little fellow. This proved to be a declaration of open war, and was so vigorously followed up that before many days the larger bird's door was not opened until his victim had had his outing and returned to his home. Teasing never lost its attraction for him, however. He delighted to alight on the cage and worry his little foe, or to stand near his door and stare at him. On one such occasion a curious scene occurred. They stood three inches apart, with the wires between them, when the finch suddenly began reaching upward as far as possible; taller and taller he stretched up, till he fairly stood on tiptoe. The mocking-bird, not to be outdone, imitated the movement on his side of the bars, of course towering far above his copy. It seemed to afford both of them great satisfaction; perhaps it expressed contempt more fully than was possible in any other way.

The largest bird in the room, a Mexican thrush, was considerably stronger and fiercer than our native wood-thrush, and it seemed absurd for the mocking-bird to measure swords with him. So it would have been but for the fact that the Mexican, having lost part of his wing feathers, was clumsy, unable to fly readily, and no match for his active, agile antagonist; he always conquered when hostilities reached the point of a personal encounter, but he was soon soured, and declined to meet the enemy. Two or three times they flew up together, like quarrelsome cocks, but the decisive and final dispute was over the bathing-dish. It happened that morning that the Mexican came out before the goldfinch was shut up, and hence the the mocking-bird's door was not yet opened. He flew at once to the top of his neighbor's cage to dress his feathers and shake himself out. It looked like a deliberate insult, and the captive in his cage evidently so regarded it; he crouched on the upper perch and opened his mouth at the enemy, who calmly went on with his operations. The moment the finch was safe at home I opened the door, and the mocking-bird came out in haste. Pretending not to see the Mexican, he descended to the bathing-dish, doubtless to cool his heated blood. The first splash, however, interested the enemy on his roof, and he flew to the floor; but the bather paid no apparent attention to him, and went on with his business. The Mexican approached slowly, a step at a time, with a low, warning "chack," which meant, "Make way there, I'm coming." The mocking-bird, manifestly hearing him, did not take the hint, nor look at his assailant, but serenely continued his splashing. The Mexican advanced to within six inches before he was convinced that force would be necessary. When he decided upon an attack, he manifested it by a grotesque little hop a few inches into the air, but this not alarming the enemy he drew near to the dish. Now at last the bather condescended to notice him. He stood up in the water and faced his adversary, bowing rather slowly and with dignity, feathers ruffled, and beak opening in the curious way usual with him,—stretching it wide, then closing it, and constantly repeating the operation.

After looking a moment at this peculiar display, the Mexican hopped upon the edge of the dish, and in the same instant, as though moved by the same machinery, the mocking-bird sprang backward out upon the floor. The usurper paid him no further attention, but proceeded to bathe, while his discomfited rival took a stand on the edge of the disputed dish, which was ten inches in diameter, and fanned his wings violently. I cannot otherwise name this extraordinary movement, the wings raised high above his head, and moved quickly back and forth with a fanning motion. The Mexican turned suddenly to him and he flew. Two or three times he repeated the performance, but was each time forced to fly before the large, strong beak wielded by his opponent, who finished his bath, and retired to a perch to dress his feathers. Now the mocking-bird resumed his splashing; but when thoroughly wet, the thought seemed to strike him that he was not in good fighting trim, and must dry himself as quickly as possible to be ready for war, which he at once did by flirting and shaking himself, bounding from one end to the other of a perch, as though he had suddenly gone mad. He was soon in order, and more than ready to resume hostilities. The enemy still occupied his favorite position upon his roof. Two cages stood side by side on a shelf, and across the tops of them, with great noise and tramping of feet, the Mexican delighted to run, thus amusing himself an hour at a time. Seeing him off his guard, the wary fellow watched his chance, and when his foe was at one end of the course he suddenly alighted on the other. The Mexican ran madly at him, clattering his bill furiously, when he gracefully rose from his place, flew over, and perched on the other end. The run was repeated, and the mischievous bird continued the annoyance until his victim was exhausted, panting, and in great excitement. From that day the Mexican gave up the contest with his too lively antagonist, and refused to come out of his cage at all; so that in fact the stranger reduced the colony to submission.

With the wood-thrush, the encounters differed from both the preceding. This bird had opened hostilities when the mocker first appeared, presuming on being the older resident, and the only bird who cared much to be on the floor. The disputed object, as already mentioned, was the apple, which they received on the matting, two pieces being placed at some distance apart. Seeing the thrush engaged with one, the mocking-bird quietly dropped to the other, when instantly the thrush deserted his own, ran hastily across the room, and claimed that piece. As he approached, the mocking-bird lifted himself into the air by a beautiful and graceful movement; he did not seem to fly, but to simply rise on wing. The thrush being occupied with that piece, the new-comer descended upon the abandoned slice; but the inhospitable bird wanted that also. Even when three or more pieces were at their disposal, the thrush tried to monopolize them all, though the plan of collecting them in one place never seemed to occur to him. After a little of this contention, the mocker generally succeeded in carrying off a bit to some quiet place, where he could eat at his leisure. Wishing them to live peaceably, I placed a slice of the fruit on a high gas-fixture, where the stranger was fond of alighting and no other bird ever went. He understood at once, flew over to it, and ate his fill. The Mexican observed this, and tramped over his cages (it was before he had retired from the world) in a rage, seeing "good times going on," and feeling, evidently, unable to fly so high. Somewhat later the thrush noticed the excitement, flew heavily up, with difficulty alighted beside the apple, snatched it off, and carried it to the floor.

Settlement of difficulties between these two birds was no chance happening; it was, to all appearance, a regularly planned campaign, and, like a savage, the aggressor put on his war paint and danced his war dance. It was extremely interesting to watch, although painful to realize that a bird could be animated by emotions so—must I call them human? He selected, for the declaration of his intentions, a moment when the thrush was in his own house and the door open. The approach to this cage was by a light ladder, the top round of which, about a foot in length, rested perhaps four inches from the cage, and level with the door. Upon this round the mocking-bird executed what has been called his war dance, shaking himself, shuffling (or moving along without raising the feet), and agitating his feathers in such a way that they rustled like stiff new silk. After a few minutes of this performance he flew away, returning presently to repeat it. This he did again and again, and his motive was plain. "You've domineered long enough," his manner said: "now come out here, and we'll settle this matter at once." The bird in the cage, though plainly surprised at this sudden exhibition of spirit, received it like a thrush—in silent dignity. He paid no attention to the demonstration further than to keep his eye upon the enemy, unless he appeared to think of entering the door, when he turned his open bill in that direction. A long time having passed in these manœuvres, the thrush, apparently tired of waiting for the belligerent to vacate his front doorstep, retired to the upper perch, and the mocking-bird immediately entered below, took his stand by the food-dish, and defied the owner, who came with open beak to dispute him, but after a few moments' silent protest returned to the high perch, leaving the intruder to eat and drink as he chose.

Another point to settle was the possession of the apple. The next time the thrush, not warned by previous operations, hurried up to claim a slice of the fruit which his foe had marked for his own, he was met by resistance. To avoid the rush, the mocking-bird lifted himself a few inches, but came down on the same spot. The thrush, astonished, but thrush-like to the last, stood motionless where he had stopped, his body drawn to a point, bill slightly open and turned toward the bold intruder. That bird ignored his attitude and placidly went on eating, and three similar experiences ended that annoyance.

One thing still remained unsettled: the mocking-bird decided to change his residence. No reason was apparent, but he preferred a special place in the room, a certain end of a particular shelf; and no matter what cage was there, he insisted on taking possession. The day he determined on this removal, he went in while the resident—the thrush—was out, and, having eaten, proceeded to the upper perches, and began jumping back and forth on them, as if at home. In due time the owner returned, visited the food-dishes, and started for the upper regions, but was met by a threatening attitude from the bird already there. He seemed to think the matter not worth quarreling over, since he readily settled himself on the middle perch, where he made a most elaborate and deliberate toilet, dressing every feather with care, and spending a half hour over the operation. All this time the invader stood on the top perch, backed against the wires, his long tail on one side like the train of a lady's dress, invincible determination in his manner. The calm indifference of the house-owner evidently did not please him, and the long drawn-out toilet was irritating; he grew thirsty, and dropped to the floor to drink, when the thrush remonstrated by a low, rapid "chook, chook, chook," and the mocking-bird made an impatient dive at him. This silenced but apparently did not hurt the bird, who stayed as long as he chose, and then quietly came out. From that moment the usurper claimed the cage, and the amiable owner easily contented himself with the one the other had deserted.

When the mocking-bird had thoroughly established himself in every right and privilege he chose to consider his own, I hoped there would be peace, but I had not sounded the depths in his character; he began to tease. Not content with complete victory, life seemed dull without some object to worry. I really think it was his amusement; he certainly went at it as if it were. I noticed him one morning, standing on the ladder before his door, apparently working himself up to something. He first looked at me,—I had a book, and pretended not to see him,—then at the thrush, who was on the floor as usual; he jerked his body this way and that, puffed out his feathers, especially on the throat and breast, held his tail on one side and turned upward at an angle of forty-five degrees, which gave him a wicked expression. He looked full of life to the tips of his toes, and greatly excited. The other birds observed him; the Mexican in his cage rustled his wings, jerked his body, and at last gave his usual cry. Even the little goldfinch was impressed and looked on with interest.

All this agitation did not escape the notice of the bird on the floor, who stood silent, plainly understanding, and waiting for the next move. Finally the mocking-bird started, gracefully and without haste. He first flew easily and lightly to the desk, in a moment to the back of a chair, then deliberately to an arm, next to the seat, and lastly to a round; at each step pausing, shaking himself, and threatening. When he reached the floor, he ran a few steps toward the thrush, stopped short, erected himself very straight, and puffed out as big as possible; then another little run, and the operation was repeated. He proceeded till within a foot of the thrush, when he alternated the upright position with a lowered head, and bill pointed toward the foe, changing from one to the other very suddenly. When he came so near, the thrush crouched flat on the floor, with beak turned squarely against the approaching bird, and thus awaited the onslaught.

In that attitude the mocking-bird did not apparently like to attack him. He threatened a long time, then retreated gradually, making feints, turning, running a few inches, and bringing up suddenly with a half turn back. In this manner he moved away for some distance, then flew to the round of the chair, the seat, the arm, the back, and so on till he reached the ladder again. Then for the first time the thrush changed his position and rose to his feet, when, without the least warning, the mocker flung himself madly after him, and the thrush, unprepared, ran, with a sharp cry. Obviously the mocking-bird, finding the first method of attack, which was probably his usual one, a failure, decided to try another, as the event proved, successfully. The excitement of this performance evidently gave him pleasure, no doubt helped to pass away the long hours, for be often indulged in it, always making his approach in the same deliberate way, tripping daintily a step or two at a time, examining everything in a careless way, tasting a piece of apple-skin, lifting a bit of thread, toying and dallying to all appearance, as he moved, still always advancing, and never turning aside from his purpose till he reached the distance of a foot from the thrush, crouching motionless with crown feathers erect. At that point he often stood a moment, looking grimly at his victim, then gave a quick, exaggerated jump which carried him forward not more than an inch, but sent the thrush, in a panic, running half across the room, where he brought up in a heap,—his claws sprawled as they slipped on the matting, every feather standing up,—and made no attempt to draw his feet together. A slow, formal attack he could meet, but a sudden rush was irresistible. Then the assailant turned, slowly, gracefully, the personification of tranquillity, his air saying, "Who's done anything?" yet taking a direct line for the enemy, approaching in the same way, by easy stages, but relentlessly drawing nearer and nearer, till he ended by a quick plunge, which sent the thrush off with a cry. In a moment he began again, teasing, following, tormenting; so wily, so wicked, so determined!

The motions of this bird were most bewitching; his flight the perfection of grace. He never flew straight across the room as if on business, but always in a dancing, loitering, easy way; hovering to examine a picture, slowly pausing on wing to look at anything, turning, wheeling, up or down or any way, buoyant and light as the air itself. It was his delight to exercise on wing about the room, diving between the rounds of the ladder, darting under a stretched string or into a cage full dash. His feet found rest on any point, however small,—the cork in a bottle, the tip of a gas-burner, or the corner post of a chair; nothing was too small or too delicately balanced for his light touch, and he never upset anything. He enjoyed running up and down a ladder six feet long with six or eight rounds, passing over it so rapidly that he could not be seen to touch it at any point, yet not using his wings he must have stepped upon every round. He always used his legs with a freedom rarely seen in a bird, not moving them together as usual in his kind, but handling them with astonishing independence of each other.

The body of this bird was capable of wonderful expression, not only in the free use of each member, but every feather seemed under his voluntary control. The spasmodic movement of the wings in excitement, common to many birds, was accomplished in an original manner by holding the wing slightly away from the body, and spreading or opening it a little at each jerk, without changing its position toward his side. His tail seemed as loosely connected with his body as if it were hung on wires; it moved even with his breathing, and the emphatic flirt of the member was an insult which every bird in the room understood. Intense interest in any sound was indicated by raising the feathers over the ears alone, which gave him the droll appearance of wearing velvet "ear muffs." In expressing other emotions he could erect the feathers of his chin, his shoulders or his back, either part alone, or all together, as he chose. A true bird of the south, he did not enjoy our climate, and if the room became too cool he made his opinion known by drawing his head down into his shoulders, with every feather on his body fluffed out, even to the base of the beak, till he looked as if wrapped in delicate gray furs to his nose, and almost burying his eyes.

The mocking-bird's emotions were so intense and so originally displayed that he was a constant source of interest. A hand-glass lying face up gave opportunity for an amusing exhibition one day. Leaning over it, he puffed out every feather, opened his mouth, and tried the glass with his beak at every point.

Meeting no satisfaction, he turned to leave it, but first peeped slyly over the edge to see if the stranger were still there, no doubt unable to get over his surprise at seeing a bird in that position and ready to meet his bill at every point. The same glass standing up brought out a different demonstration. He stood in front of it and swelled himself out, while the feathers of the shoulders and breast were erected. Then he opened his mouth wide and attacked the reflection, but was astonished to meet the glass. He touched the bill of his double with his own, and moved all the way to the bottom of the glass, not taking it away, but apparently trying to seize the one which opposed his. He lowered his head as though to take hold of the enemy's foot, then pulled himself up as straight as a soldier, wings and tail constantly jerking with excitement. After indulging for some time in these proceedings, he dodged around behind the glass, plainly expecting to pounce upon his opponent, and surprised not to do so. Several times he drew himself up, swelled out his breast, and blustered before the glass. Once he flew up with the reflection in the manner of a quarrelsome cock, and upon reaching the top of the glass, naturally went over and landed behind, without an enemy in sight. Upon this he stared a moment, as if dazed, then shook himself out, and flew away in evident disgust.

The deliberate, leisurely dressing of plumage, with which many birds pass away the dull hours, is an occupation in which the mocking-bird never had time to indulge. He was a bird of affairs; he had too much on his mind for loitering. A few sudden, thorough shakes, a rapid snatching of the wing and tail feathers through the beak, or, after a bath, a violent beating the air with both wings while holding tightly to the perch with his feet, sufficed for his toilet. Notwithstanding his apparent carelessness, his plumage was soft and exquisite in texture, and when wet the downy breast feathers matted together and hung in locks, like hair. Through a common magnifying glass each tiny barbule was seen to be ringed with gray and silvery white, so finely that the rings could hardly be seen.

The most beautiful and peculiar attitude this bird assumed was when conducting an attack upon a small object. Seeing one day a steel pen-point black with ink, he stood before it at a respectful distance, and raised both wings over his back till they almost touched each other, holding the tail on one side. In two or three seconds he lowered the wings a moment, then raised them again, while his tail leaned the other side. After half a dozen such feints he delivered a gentle peck, and instantly hopped back out of the way. Seeing that it did not move, he took it in his bill and flew to the floor, where he soon satisfied himself that it was not a new variety of beetle. This was always his method with any new object of small size.

Not only did this doughty warrior vanquish the ordinary birds about him, but when a gray African parrot made his appearance in the room (on a short visit) he boldly attacked him, in spite of his size and strength. The parrot had a temporary perch before the window, and on the cage nearest to him the mocking-bird took his place, and after posturing and threatening, stooped to a crouching position, and then darted past him, trying to hit him as he went. The first time this occurred the parrot whirled on his perch and cried "Whoo!" and after that greeted every charge with a very good imitation of a policeman's rattle, probably as the loudest and most terrifying noise he could make. So determined was the belligerent fellow to subdue or annihilate the larger bird, and so reckless were his attacks, that I had to keep him a prisoner during the few days the parrot was in the room, for hospitality must not be violated. It is interesting to note that so great was his variety of resource that he had a distinctly different method of warfare in each of the six cases mentioned.

A dignified composure was so natural to my bird that he was never startled out of it, not even when suddenly enveloped in a shawl, a proceeding that greatly alarms birds of less self-possession. It was necessary on one occasion to catch him to return him to his cage, where he might be protected from the cold of the night. All the usual ways were tried without success, so lightly did he slip away, so gracefully and calmly did he flutter around the room, not in the least disturbed or confused by the darkness, and quite willing to play hide-and-seek all night. No other way availing, the last resource was tried—throwing a shawl over him as he stood crouched on the top of the cage, ready for instant flight. Not a flutter nor a cry arose, and it seemed that he must have escaped; but on looking through the cage from below, he was seen flattened against the wires, but perfectly quiet, submissive to the inevitable, like any other philosopher. He was gathered up in the folds and carefully uncovered before his own door, when he simply hopped to a perch and coolly returned the gaze of his captors, not a feather out of place, not in the smallest degree disconcerted.

Amusements were not lacking in this interesting life aside from the pleasures of worrying and teasing, which plainly were entertainments for him. He indulged in other performances which distinctly were play. Especially was this true of the habit he imitated from the Mexican,—tramping across two cages heavily, with as much noise as possible, and then with an extravagant jump landing on another cage, where he was received with a scolding, which apparently pleased him as much as any part of it. A specially quick flying-run rattled a paper fastened against the wall, which delighted him greatly; and when the cages were covered with paper, to put an end to the proceeding which annoyed the residents, he regarded it as a particular attention, and enjoyed it more than ever, doubtless because it enabled him to make a louder noise. Often he diverted himself by a mad frolic in his cage; from place to place he went half flying, and scarcely touching anything; back and forth, with great flutter of wings and great noise; up and down, under and over and around his perches, in the same wild way, so that it seemed as if he must beat his brains out. Then suddenly, when most riotous, he alighted like a feather, the image of serenity and repose. Sometimes he was seized with this sort of fury of play when out of his cage, and then he flung himself about the room in the same frantic manner, scarcely touching a perch, diving under a table, between the rounds of a chair, over a gas-fixture, behind and through any openings he could find. Should some bird in the room disapprove of this behavior, and scold, as the finch was quite apt to do, the mocking-bird instantly alighted beside him, humped his back till he looked deformed, sidled two or three steps towards him, stopped, and stared at his critic; then two or three steps more, stopping again, and in every way acting more like a mischievous monster than a bird, till the astonished finch was reduced to silence, and as meek as poor Mrs. Quilp before the antics of her malicious little spouse.

In all these actions, even in his contests with his room-mates, no anger ever appeared on the part of the mocking-bird; everything seemed done to amuse himself and pass away the weary hours, rather than from desire to hurt his neighbors. In fact, he never did positively touch a bird, to my knowledge, though he always acted as though he intended to annihilate them. He could hardly be called malicious; rather (shall we say?) mischievous, and like Ariel "a tricksy spirit."

THE "WISE BLUEBIRD."

Never was sweeter music—
Sunshine turned into song.
To set us dreaming of summer,
When the days and the dreams are long.
Winged lute that we call a bluebird,
You blend in a silver strain
The sound of the laughing waters,
The patter of spring's sweet rain,
The voice of the wind, the sunshine,
And fragrance of blossoming things.
Ah! you are a poem of April,
That God endowed with wings.
Eben. E. Rexford.

V.

THE "WISE BLUEBIRD."

"A wise bluebird
Puts in his little heavenly word."

The characteristic air and expression of the bluebird, and his enchanting little warble, could not be better described in a page of writing than the poet has here done in a couplet.

Who has not seen him in his favorite resting-place, the lowest branch of an apple-tree, standing up very straight, crown feathers erected, honest little countenance squarely facing one, motionless and silent, looking the embodiment of wisdom!

A pair of bluebirds lived in my house for nearly a year, and the calm, imposing manner of the male I have never seen disturbed. In the presence of birds much larger than himself he never lost his equanimity, paid not the slightest attention to any one, went about his daily duties and pleasures exactly as though there were not another bird, except his mate, in the room. Quite otherwise was his little spouse: quick, nervous, easily frightened, yet assuming the responsibility of everything, even her lord's comfort and safety. Her very attitude was different; she held her body horizontal, never perpendicular, as he did; and she was more lively in movement. She was a brave little soul, too. Even when greatly annoyed by a larger bird, she never failed to stand upon the defensive, open her mouth, and sometimes remonstrate in low, gentle talk. Nor did she—after she felt at home—allow a stranger to enter her door. She boldly faced the largest bird in the room, and always forced him to retire, while her mate stood calm and cool and "wise," on the upper perch. More than this, she seemed to feel it part of her duty to defend and protect his lordship, as though he were too fragile to come into contact with the rough side of life. Nothing could be droller than to see her stand guard while he bathed in the common dish on the table, and fly furiously at the grosbeak, or any bird coming too near her precious idol, who meanwhile placidly proceeded with his bath in the most matter-of-fact manner, as though expecting to be protected. I have seen similar conduct in a wild pair: the female defending her nestlings against some fancied danger, scolding, flying around the intruder, and taking the whole care upon herself; while her spouse occupied the topmost twig of the tree on which his family was in trouble, uttering at short intervals his musical cry of distress, one rich, loud note.

I did, however, on one occasion see a male bluebird excited in the defense of his young. It was in North Carolina, where a nestling chanced to alight on the favorite resting-place of a mocking-bird, and the latter a moment afterward came to his usual perch not a foot from the wild-eyed youngster. Then arose a great outcry from both bluebirds, and one after the other swooped down at that mocking-bird, coming so near I thought they must hit him. Again and again they returned to the charge with loud cries, while the mocking-bird stood quiet, crouched as though to dash into the little one, and jerking wings and tail in a wicked manner. It lasted but a moment, for the nestling itself was scared and flew to another branch, upon which the attack came to an end, and the mother went to the baby, but the father stood on a perch near the enemy, and scolded for some time.

Perhaps this individual bluebird had learned to assist in the family defense, for they had other troubles. The nest was in an unsafe spot, the hollow dead limb of a tall pine-tree, about seventy feet above the ground. The opening was in the lower side of the sloping branch, making it very easy for a nestling to fall out, and that is what I think happened the day before the little scene above described.

Hearing cries of distress from the pine grove, I hastened down to see if I could be of any assistance. Both bluebirds were on a low tree, about a foot apart, uttering constantly the mournful notes I had heard. Evidently a tragedy of some sort had occurred, and I thought at once of a falling little one. I looked carefully around the tree while the parents came down near me, much disturbed. I found nothing, but a gale was blowing and a little bird might easily have been driven far away. It was a serious matter plainly, for the cries went on without intermission the rest of the day.

During that time I saw a curious and interesting attempt at consolation on the part of the male. He flew away, and returned in a few moments with something in his beak. Alighting near his mate, he began a low, tender twitter, at the same time offering the morsel to her. She moved a few inches away; he followed, still coaxing. She flew to another branch, refusing to look at it. He followed, still asking her to accept it. At last she flew away, and he seemed astounded, stood as if he did not know what to do next, hesitated several minutes, when a bright thought seemed to strike him, and he carried it to the nest.

The pair in my room were a most affectionate and gentle couple; no disputes, not even the smallest difference, arose between them. If one wished to bathe while the other was using the bath-tub, he stood on the edge till his turn came. In the same way one usually waited for the other to finish a lunch before going down himself, though on rare occasions they descended together for a social meal. If she were alarmed, and went to the floor, as at first sometimes happened, he at once appeared in the door, looking anxiously after her, and calling tenderly. If she did not return, he flew down himself, ran about till he found her, and, after talking in a low tone for some time, started for home, when she followed him, showing that she was reassured. They always sat on the same perch, and on cool days as near each other as possible, first one and then the other "hitching" a little nearer. After bathing they sunned themselves together, even when in the cage, where the sunshine came only into one corner, and they crowded so closely that there was not room to spread out. Even that discomfort never elicited a harsh word, though he enjoyed spreading himself very completely, bending his legs, resting his breast on the floor, and opening his wings to their full extent.

This bird's anxiety when his mate was out of his sight did not, however, compare with her unrest in his absence, for her affection seemed to be of the motherly or protecting sort. Before they became familiar with the room, and learned that, though unseen, the partner was not lost, the moment he disappeared from view she began running around the cage excitedly, looking everywhere, and calling loudly. At first he answered, but, deciding to try his wings, he swept around the room, came—as some birds do—against the window, and fell to the floor, when instantly both were perfectly silent. She looked out apprehensively, and as soon as he recovered breath he flew to the top of their own cage. Then her solicitude turned to annoyance; she went to the top perch, and gently nipped his toes (which she never did to strangers) as a slight reproof. He became accustomed to going out and in sooner than his mate, for she was shy and inclined to stay at home, and she suffered much anxiety; before long she too grew accustomed to freedom, and expressed no further fears when he was out.

Making arrangements for the night was an interesting event in bluebird life. They always selected the highest perch in the darkest end of the cage, and placed themselves so close together that they looked like a wide ball, or two balls that had been almost pressed into one when in a very soft state. In the morning the feathers on the side next the mate were crushed flat, requiring much shaking and dressing to give them their ordinary appearance. What was curious, the female took the outside, no doubt with the motherly motive of taking care of him. To see them settle themselves was pleasing. Being more quiet and less nervous than his spouse, the singer generally retired first, some time before she was ready, and composed himself in a moment in his corner, for they were never restless at evening; she followed when she chose. Occasionally, however, she went first, taking her place about as far as usual from the wires, and leaving space for him. But if he went to his place, there was not room to turn around, facing the middle of the cage, as was their custom; and he seemed to appreciate the difficulty, for he hopped up on the outside, or the wrong side of her. Instantly she jumped to a lower perch, when he sidled up to his regular place, and she at once returned and took her usual position beside him. One night something startled them, and both flew wildly around the cage. I produced a light to show them the perches, so they might quiet themselves again. The male readily did so, but she remained on the lower perch. I went close to the wires and began to speak soothingly, to calm her, and induce her to resume her place, when, to my surprise, she began to reply to me, every time I spoke, standing less than a foot from me. She stared me full in the face, not at all disturbed, and answered every word I said with her musical call, in a low tone, as if to tell me the story of the fright. We kept up the queer little chat for several minutes, and she did not return to his side that night.

One advantage of studying two birds of a kind at the same time is to observe the talk between them, which has great interest for me. This pair were exceedingly talkative at first, uttering not only the usual musical three-syllable warble or call, which Lanier aptly calls the "heavenly word," but often soft twittering prattle, of varying inflection and irregular length, which was certainly the most interesting bird-talk I ever heard. When they could not see me they indulged in it more freely, with changing tones at different times, and after they became accustomed to the room and its inhabitants it was neither so frequent nor so earnest. Often at night, when one—perhaps in a dream—fell off the perch, I heard much low, tender talk, almost in a whisper, before all was quiet again; and when another bird flew wildly around the room, there was always a remark or two in an interested tone. The male did most of the talking, carrying on, often for a long time, a constant flow of what sounded marvelously like comments and criticisms, while his mate replied occasionally with the usual call. Certain notes plainly had a specific meaning, even to the others in the room. One in particular was peculiar and low, but upon its utterance every bird became instantly silent and looked at the cage, while the bluebirds themselves were so absorbed, gazing apparently into blank space, that I could easily put my hands on them before they observed me. For several minutes this low note would be repeated, and all the birds stare at nothing, till I began to feel almost uncomfortable, as I have done at similar staring at nothing on the part of animals. One can hardly resist the feeling that these creatures can see something invisible to our eyes. On one occasion, when the male uttered this note, the female was just about to eat; she stood as if petrified, with head halfway down to the food, for two or three minutes.

What I have called talk was a very low twitter in a conversational tone, on one note, not at all in a singing tone, like the usual warble or call. I have also heard it from wild bluebirds, when I could get near enough. From the first, as said above, the male did most of the talking, and the habit grew upon him, till he became a regular babbler, standing on the top perch, and keeping it up persistently all day long. I think it arose from the fact that the greater number of birds in the room were thrushes, who sang very softly, without opening the mouth. With this gentle ripple of song the bluebird's voice harmonized perfectly, and he almost entirely discontinued his lovely song, while indulging himself in talk by the hour. Strange to say, I soon noticed that his mate did not approve of it, and would not stand on the perch beside him while he continued it. At first she turned sharply towards him, and he showed that he understood her wishes by ceasing for a while; but as the habit grew, and he was not so easily silenced, she more and more deserted his side, and after two or three weeks I heard occasionally a gentle remonstrance from her. I do not believe a really harsh tone can come from a bluebird throat. One day they were taking their usual midday nap on the same perch, when a thrush across the window began his low song. That started the bluebird, and he added his chatter, which awakened his mate. She endured it for about five seconds, and then she suddenly stretched the wing nearest him so far that he was obliged to move away, when she instantly hopped down herself.

The two bluebirds differed in intelligence. The female was quicker to take an idea, but the male sooner conquered his fear. The first time I offered meal-worms to them she was so lively as to secure more than her share; but he learned in a day or two that worms were to be had outside, especially on my desk, when he at once flew over to me and demanded them, in the funniest little defiant way, looking at me most significantly, and wiping his bill ostentatiously, then jerking himself with great show of impatience. Words could not be plainer. Neither of them had difficulty in telling me their food-dish was empty; they stood on the edge and looked at me, then scraped the bill several times, making much noise about it, then looked at me again. I knew in a moment, the first time, what they wanted. When the male found out that another bird alighted on a stick I held out to him, and was carried off upon it, he seemed to be seized with curiosity, and the next time I offered it he jumped upon it beside the other, and allowed himself to be lifted to the desk. At one time, in flying around, he caught his feet in the coarse net curtains I hung before the windows to keep strange birds from trying to fly out. I went at once to him and took him off. He scolded, fluttered, and pecked, and, when I had released him, flew directly against another curtain and caught again. I went over to him, and this time he understood that I was helping him; he neither struggled nor pecked, and flew quietly when I set him free.

The bluebird never showed any curiosity about the room or the world outside the windows, but sat on his door perch for hours, with a sharp eye to the worm supply. The appearance of the cup that held them was a signal for him to come down and beg for them, but his little mate never dared trust herself on the desk, though when I threw a worm on the floor she invariably secured it. So fond was she of this delicacy that she once played a saucy trick upon a scarlet tanager. Having received a worm, he went into the first open door he saw,—which happened to be the bluebird's,—to find a place to manipulate the morsel, which he never swallowed whole. Madam stood on the perch just above the entrance, and as he came in she leaned over and snatched it out of his mouth, swallowed it, wiped her bill, and turned to him, ready for another. His stare of blank amazement was amusing to see, but he quickly made up his mind that it was not a safe place to eat, and when I gave him another he went to the roof of the same cage. She instantly mounted the top perch, put up her bill and seized the worm; but he held on, dragged it away, and then retired to his own cage with it. She positively could not resist this temptation, and even from her own cherished spouse she would sometimes snatch the desired tidbit.

The bluebirds' method of bathing differed from any I have noticed. They put the head under water, and held it there, while spattering vigorously with wings and tail. On leaving the bath the female fanned herself dry, holding tightly to the perch and beating her wings with violence, while dancing back and forth the whole length of the perch, in a bewitching manner. Her mate fanned himself also, adding a very pretty lateral shake of the wings, and raising the feathers on the crown and throat till he looked twice as big as usual. But he was very fond of sunning himself dry, in the attitude already spoken of. That position, by the way, was a not unusual one with him; he often hopped the length of three feet before a blind which stood against the wall, his legs bent, head nearly touching the floor, and tail thrust almost straight up. A droll figure he made. After hopping to the end of the blind, he would dash around behind it, as if he expected or hoped to find something.

After moulting, the birds feathered out beautifully, and their spirits rose in proportion. They delighted in flight, making long, sweeping circles around the room, again and again, without stopping. A few weeks later, as spring approached, they grew somewhat belligerent towards the other inhabitants of the place; driving every bird away from their cage, even following them to their chosen resting-places, insisting on their right to every perch in the room. Then, too, began signs of courtship between the lovely pair. The first thing I noticed was at worm-feeding time. One day I had given each of them their portion. The female swallowed hers instantly, and I turned to another cage, when I heard a low, coaxing cry many times repeated. I looked around. The male stood on the upper perch, still holding his worm, which he usually dispatched as quickly as his mate did hers; and she was on a lower perch, looking up at him, mouth open, wings fluttering, asking for it. While I looked, he hopped down beside her, she opened her mouth wide, and he fed her as if she were a nestling. He was more amiable than a wild bluebird I once saw, who had brought up a long earthworm, and was beating it on top of a post preparatory to swallowing it, when his little spouse—who was sitting at the time—came to the fence rail below him, and asked in the same way for a bit. So far from sharing it with her, this greedy bird simply took a fresh hold of his prize, flew to a tree, and gobbled it down with difficulty himself. Not so my generous captive. The next day he complied with her request again, and after that it was he who did the tender coaxing, begging her to accept the slight offering of his love. Soon, too, she grew coquettish in manner, often turned a cold shoulder to him, opened her mouth at him, and scolded in the sweetest and softest voice; and one night, after they had settled on their perch, I heard gentle talk, and saw a little peck or two on her part. He did the talking, and she delivered the playful peck or push as reply. Now, too, in his desire to manifest his affection, he could not always wait for worms, but picked dainty bits from the food-dish, and tendered them in the same pretty way. She always accepted, though often she went at once to the food-dish and ate for herself; for with all this sentiment and love-making her appetite did not fail. Once she was outside and he inside the cage, when he began to call and offer her something out of his mouth. She did not wish to go in, so she flew to a perch that ran through the cage, and stood close to the wires, while he went to the same perch inside, and fed her through the wires.

About this time, too, the bluebird talk nearly ceased, and instead of it the lovely song of three notes was heard all day, and a little change they made in it—throwing in a "grace note" between the second and third—greatly added to its charm. Now, too, spring had really come, and I waited only for warm days to let them go and set up their homestead in freedom. The first mild day in May the window was opened for them. The female flew first to a tree in front of the house, where she was greeted in the rudest manner by the bird-tramps which infest our streets,—the house-sparrows. They began to assemble around her, no doubt prepared for attack, when she gave a loud cry of distress, and out flew her valiant knight to her aid. After a moment's pause by her side, they both flew, and we saw the gentle pair no more.

This true chronicle began with a quotation from Lanier; it shall end with one from Harriet Prescott Spofford:—

"A bit of heaven itself, he flew,

When earth seemed heaven with bees and bloom,

South wind, and sunshine, and perfume;

And morning were not morn without him.

Winging, springing, always flinging,

Flinging music all about him."

THE GOLDEN-WING.

The high-hole flashing his golden wings.
Walt Whitman.

VI.

THE GOLDEN-WING.

One of the special objects of my search during a certain June among the hills of northern New York was a nest of the golden-winged woodpecker; not that it is rare or hard to find, but because I had never seen one and had read attractive stories of the bird's domestic relations, the large number of young in the nest, and his devotion and pride. Moreover, I had become greatly interested in the whole family, through my attachment to an individual member of it in my own house.

I soon discovered that the orchard at the back of the house was visited every day by a pair of the birds I was seeking. One was seen running up and down a trunk of a large poplar-tree, and the next morning two alighted on a dead branch at the top of an apple-tree, perching like other birds on twigs, which seemed too light to bear their weight. But they were apparently satisfied with them; for they stayed some time, pluming themselves and evidently looking with interest and astonishment at human intruders into what had no doubt been a favorite haunt of their own. I watched them for several minutes, till a sudden noise startled the shy creatures and they were off in an instant.

After that I saw them often at the bottom of the orchard. They always flew over the place with rather a heavy business-like flight, alighted on a low branch of the farthest apple-tree, and in a moment dropped to the ground where the long grass hid them. There they remained five minutes or more before returning to the tree. Unfortunately it was a little farther than I could readily see with my glass, and the most cautious approach alarmed them. I heard them call nearly every day in loud, strong voice, "Pe-auk! pe-auk!"

Being thus baffled in my plan of following them home, I resolved upon a regular search in the small piece of woods where they always disappeared, and every morning I spent two or three hours in that lovely spot looking for any birds, but especially for the Golden-wing. In all my search, however, I found but one nest, which may have been his, where apparently a tragedy had occurred; for from the edge of the opening the bark was torn off down the trunk, and in two or three places holes were picked as though to reach the nest which had been within.

Whatever the drama enacted in that mysterious home, I was too late to see, and I have not been able as yet to make close acquaintance with the free Golden-wing.

The bird that had so interested me in his whole family I found in a bird store in New York in the month of November. He was a most disconsolate-looking object, and so painfully wild I could scarcely bear to look at him—poor, shy, frightened soul, set up in a cage to be stared at. I rescued him at once with the intention of giving him a more retired home, and freedom the moment spring opened. The change did not at first reassure him, and he was so frantic that his cage was covered to shut out the sights till he was accustomed to the sounds of a household. Gradually, an inch or two at a time, the cover that hid the world from him was reduced, till at the end of three weeks he could endure the removal of the last corner without going absolutely mad.

On the first day an opening a few inches wide was left in his screen, so that he might look out if he chose, and I took my seat as far as possible from him, with my back to him, and a hand-glass so arranged that I could see him. As soon as the room was quiet he went to the opening and cautiously thrust his long bill and his head as far as the eye beyond the edge so that he could see me. I kept perfectly still, while he watched me several minutes with evident interest, and I was glad to see that it was simply fright and not idiocy that caused his panics.

Many emotions of the bird were most comically expressed by hammering. In embarrassment or alarm, when not so great as to drive him wild, he resorted to that diversion, and the more disturbed, the louder and faster his blows. If in utter despair, as when I set his house in order for the day, he dropped to the floor on the farthest side, put his head in the corner, and pounded the tray with great violence. Every wire in the cage in turn he tested with taps of his beak, thus amusing himself hours at a time, sitting, as was his custom, crouched upon the perch or on the floor. In this way, too, he tried the quality of the plastered wall behind his cage, and was evidently pleased to find it yielding, for he bored many holes and tore off much paper, before he was discovered and provided with a background of wood to exercise upon.

The unhappy bird had a serious time learning to eat mocking-bird food with his long, curved beak; he never became very expert at it, but was as awkward as a child learning to feed itself. He first thrust it like a dagger its whole length into his dish, took out a mouthful, then turned his head sidewise, shook it and snapped his bill one side and the other, making a noise as if choking. When this performance was over, he scraped his beak against the wires and picked off the fragments daintily with the tip. When he had eaten he left a straight, smooth hole in the food, like a stab, two inches deep and perhaps half an inch in diameter. In drinking he made the same movements, filling his mouth, throwing back his head, and swallowing with great efforts.

All of the Golden-wing's attitudes were peculiar; as, for instance, he never liked to face one, but always turned his back upon spectators and looked at them over his shoulder. In sleeping he changed his position often, and was as restless as a nervous old man. Sometimes he slept on the perch, puffed out into a ball like other birds, head buried in his feathers, tail broad-spread and curled under the perch, as though it needed something to rest against. If he began his night's rest (or unrest) in this position, in a few hours he would drop heavily to the floor, scramble about a little, and then climb to one of the supports that kept the wires in place, ten inches from the bottom of the cage. There he settled himself comfortably, head buried again, tail pressed against the wires, and looking more like a spot on the wall than a bird.

He often took naps in the daytime on the floor with his head in the corner, like a bad boy in punishment, his head drawn down into his shoulders and his bill thrust up into the air at an angle of forty-five degrees. If this tired him, he simply turned his bill down at about the same angle, and tried it that way awhile.

44

He was an exceedingly early bird, always settled to sleep long before any other in the room, and he slept very soundly, being not easily wakened and breathing in long, steady respirations like a person in sleep. Indeed he startled me very much the first time I noticed him. The breathing was regular and strong, equal in duration to my own as I listened, and I was sure some one was in the room. I hastened to light the gas to look for the burglar, and it was not until I had made thorough search that I discovered who was the guilty one. He dreamed also, if one may judge by the sounds that came from his cage at night, complaining, whining, almost barking like the "yaps" of a young puppy, and many sorts of indescribable noises.

The Golden-wing was extremely fond of hanging against the side of his cage on the support spoken of above. Not only did he sleep in that position, but dress his plumage, turning his head back over his body and sides, and even arranging the feathers of his breast, each one by itself, with scrupulous care. Like many others this bird objected to having his cage used as a perch by his neighbors. He expressed his sentiments by quick jerks, first of the shoulders and then of the whole body, and if the intruder did not take the hint, he opened his enormous bill and took hold of a stray toe, which usually drove away the most impertinent.

The door of the cage was opened to my captive as soon as he became quiet and happy within it. After his first surprise and dismay at finding himself in the big world again, he enjoyed it very much. Being unable to fly through the loss of some wing feathers, his cage was placed on the floor, and he ran in and out at pleasure. He was more than usually intelligent about it, too; for although the door was small, and he had to lower his head to pass through, he was never at a loss for an instant.

One thing that shows a bird's characteristics and that I have never seen any two do in exactly the same way, is to explore a room when first released from a cage. This bird, like his predecessors, had his own peculiar notion, which was to go behind everything. He squeezed himself between a trunk, or a heavy piece of furniture, and the wall, where it did not seem possible that one of his size could pass, and showed so great an inclination to go through a hole in the open-work fire-board that I hastily covered it up. After a while he tested the matting and carefully investigated, by light taps of his bill, each separate nail. His step was heavy, and he did not hop, but ran around with a droll little patter of the feet, like a child's footsteps.

Having exhausted the novelty of the floor, he turned his eyes upward, perhaps noticing that the other birds were higher in the room, where they had taken refuge when he made his sudden and somewhat alarming appearance among them. He did not try to fly, but he was not without resources; he could jump, and no one could outdo him in climbing, or in holding on. After a moment's apparent consideration of the means at his command, he ran to the corner and mounted a trunk by springing up halfway, holding on a moment in some mysterious manner, and then by a second jump landing on top. From that point it was easy to reach the bird's table, and there was a ladder placed for the benefit of another that could not fly. This ladder he at once pounced upon, and used as if he had practiced on one all his life.

I shut the cage-door at the upper end to keep him out of his neighbor's house, while the owner, an American wood-thrush, stood upon the roof, looking ruefully at this appropriation of his private property. Upon reaching the closed door the traveler jumped across to another cage nearly a foot away. This was a small affair occupied by an English goldfinch, who was then at home and not pleased by the call, as he at once made known. Golden-wing, however, perhaps with the idea of returning past insults from the saucy little finch, jerked himself all around the cage, inserting his long bill as though trying to reach something inside.

Having wearied of annoying the enemy, he sprang back to the ladder, descended by the table and trunk to the floor as he had gone up, without a moment's hesitation as to the way, which proved him to possess unusual intelligence. He did not take the trouble to climb down, but put his two feet together and jumped heavily like a child, a very odd movement for a bird. It was his constant habit in the cage to jump from the perch to the floor, and from one that was two inches above the tray he often stepped down backwards, which I never before saw a bird do.

When after three hours of exploration he returned to his home, the door was closed and the cage hung up. He was satisfied with his first outing, and refreshed himself with a nap at once. But the first thing the next morning he came down to his door and pecked the wires, looking over at me most intelligently, plainly asking to have it opened. He never mistook the position of the door, and if knocking had not the desired effect, he took hold of a wire and shook and rattled it till he was attended to.

It was interesting to see how familiar he suddenly became, when no effort had been made to induce him to be so. I never had so much trouble to win the confidence of a bird, but when won, the surrender was complete. He came up to me freely and allowed me to catch him in my hand without resistance, which is very uncommon. (Perhaps I ought to say that I do not try to tame my birds.) He displayed a child-like, confiding disposition, both in his unreasoning terror at first, and his unquestioning faith at last.

These investigations were conducted without a sound, for the bird was entirely silent while awake. But there came a day when he made a curious exhibition of his ability. It was the ninth of February, and the goldfinch was calling, as he often did. The woodpecker sat on his perch with wings held tightly against his sides, "humped" up as though he were high-shouldered. The plumage of his breast was puffed out so broadly that it came over the wings, and in a front view completely hid them, while the feathers of his shoulders were erected till he resembled a lady with a fur shoulder cape. Withal, his head was drawn down to his body, and his beak pointed upward at an angle of forty-five degrees. In this peculiar and absurd position he began a strange little song, ludicrously weak and low for a bird of his size. The tones were delivered in a sharp staccato style, like "picking" the strings of a violin very softly, several notes uttered with queer sidewise jerks of the head, and eyes apparently fixed on the goldfinch. After a phrase or two he scraped his bill violently and then began again.

This performance he varied by bowing his head many times, swaying his whole body from side to side, flirting his tail and shaking his wings. It was an extraordinary display, but whether his manner of making himself agreeable, or of expressing contempt, I could only guess. The goldfinch looked on with interest, though I think he understood it no better than I did; he seemed surprised, but rather pleased, for he repeated his calls, and the Golden-wing kept up the strange exhibition for some time.

I became greatly attached to my beautiful bird, which appeared, in the presence of his wise and wary room-mates, cat-birds and thrushes, like a big, clumsy, but affectionate baby. It was solely on his account and principally, I must confess, to try and surprise a wild bird at the above described entertainment so as to determine its character, that I wished to make acquaintance with its free relations, study their ways when at liberty in their own haunts, and have a glimpse if possible of the Golden-wing babies.

A year later I had the opportunity I so much desired of making acquaintance with the young of this family. I was sitting one morning on the edge of a deep ravine filled with trees, deeply engaged in the study of another bird, when suddenly a stranger came with an awkward flop against the trunk of a tree not ten feet from me. I saw in an instant that it was the infant I had looked for so long. He was exactly like the parents, with a somewhat shorter tail. I should hardly have suspected his youthfulness but for his clumsy movements, and the fact that he did not at once take flight, which a Golden-wing more experienced in the ways of human-kind would have done instantly. He seemed somewhat exhausted by his flight, and clung to the trunk, with soft dark eyes fixed upon me, ready to move if I did.

I did not; I sat motionless for half an hour and watched him. When somewhat rested he dodged around the other side of the trunk, and peeped at me through a fork in the branches. Then he scrambled upon a small branch, where he perched crosswise. But he had trouble to keep his balance in that position, so he climbed about till he found a limb fully two inches in diameter, on which he could rest in the favorite flicker attitude—lengthwise. Then with his head outward to the world at large, and his tail turned indifferently toward me,—whom he doubtless regarded as a permanent and lifeless feature of the landscape,—he settled himself, crouched flat against the bark, for a comfortable nap.

All this time I had been conscious of low Golden-wing talk about me; the familiar "wick-up! wick-up!" almost in a whisper, a softened "pe-auk!" from the ravine, and the more distant "laugh," so called. The infant on the tree heard too. He moved his head, listened and looked, but whether or not they were words of caution and advice from the wiser ones of his race, he refused to be frightened and did not move till I rose to leave him, when, greatly startled, he took flight across the ravine.

A STORMY WOOING.

Not an inch of his body is free from delight,
Can he keep himself still if he would? Oh, not he!
The music stirs in him like wind through a tree.
Wordsworth.

VII.

A STORMY WOOING.

If, as Ruskin says, "the bird is little more than a drift of the air, brought into form by plumes," the particular bit shaped into the form we call the orchard oriole must be a breath from a Western tornado, for a more hot-headed, blustering individual would be hard to find; and when this embodied hurricane, this "drift" of an all-destroying tempest, goes a-wooing, strange indeed are the ways he takes to win his mate, and stranger still the fact that he does win her in spite of his violence.

In a certain neighborhood, where I spent some time in the nesting season, studying a bird of vastly different character, orchard orioles were numerous, and in their usual fashion made their presence known by persistent singing around the house. For it must be admitted, whatever their defects of temper or manners, that they are most cheerful in song, the female no less than the male. First of the early morning bird chorus comes their song, loud, rich, and oft-repeated, though marred in the case of the male by the constant interpolation of harsh, scolding notes. Anywhere, everywhere, all day, in pouring rain, in high wind that silences nearly every bird voice, the orioles sing. One could not overlook them if he wished, so noisy, so restless, and so musical. Nor do they care to be unseen; they make no attempt at concealment. No oriole ever steals into a neighborhood in the quiet way of the cat-bird, silently taking an observation of its inhabitants before making himself obvious; on the contrary, all his deeds are before the public, even his family quarrels. He comes to a tree with a bustle, talking, scolding, making himself and his affairs the most conspicuous things in the neighborhood.

Many times he is most annoying. When following some shy bird to its nest, or moving down toward the grove where are the brooklet and the birds' bathing-place, no matter how quietly one may approach, footsteps deadened by thick sand and no rustling garments to betray, the orchard oriole is sure to know it. He is not the only bird to see a stranger, of course; the brown thrush is as quick as he, but he silently drops to the ground, if not already there, and disappears without a sound; the cardinal grosbeak slips down from his perch on the farther side and takes wing near the ground; the cat-bird, in the center of a thick shrub, noiseless as a shadow, flutters across the path and is gone; others do the same. The orchard oriole alone shouts the news to all whom it may concern in his loudest "chack! chack!" putting every one on his guard at once, and making the copse in a moment as empty as though no wing ever stirred its leaves.

On first noticing the ways of the birds about me on the occasion mentioned, I saw that there was some sort of a disturbance among them; scarcely ten minutes passed without a commotion, followed by a chase through the branches of a tree, one bird pursuing another so hotly that twigs bent and leaves parted as they passed, the one in advance often uttering a complaining cry, and the pursuer, a loud, harsh scold. Something exciting was evidently going on; some tragedy or possibly comedy, in this extremely sensational family. I was at once interested to see what it might be and how it would end; and in fact, before I knew it, I was as much absorbed in oriole matters as though no other feathered life was to be seen.

There were in the party two males, one in his second year, and therefore immature in coloring, being olive-yellow on the breast, brown on wings and tail, with a black mask over eyes and chin; the other was older, and a model of oriole beauty, being bright chestnut on the lower parts, with velvety black hood coming down on the breast. With them was one female, and though far from being friends, the three were never separated. The trouble seemed to be that both males were suitors, and notwithstanding the pretty little maid appeared to have a mind of her own and to prefer the younger of her wooers, the older plainly refused "to take no for an answer," and was determined to have his own way, bringing to bear on his courtship all the persistence of his race. In that particular quality of never giving up what he has set his heart on, the oriole cannot be excelled, if indeed he can be equaled in the bird world; for a time, and a long time, too, he is a bird of one idea, and by fair means or foul he will almost certainly accomplish his desire, whatever it may be.

Life never grew dull in the party mentioned; they were always talking, singing, or going for each other in the mad way already described. Sometimes the chase was between the males, but oftener the female flew for her life apparently, while the rough wooer followed closely with great noise and confusion. The affair ended occasionally with a cry of distress as though somebody was pecked, but several times she stood at bay and defied him with mouth open, feathers bristled up, wings fluttering, and every way quite ready to defend herself. Like other blusterers, on the first show of fight he calmed down, and the matter ended for the time. Peace lasted from ten to twenty minutes, during which they hopped about the tree, or hung head-downward on the Spanish moss, talking in low tones, though the male never omitted delivering a scolding note with every two or three pleasant ones. Her voice was charming, in a tender call, a gentle chatter, or a sweet song, unspoiled by the harsh tones of her partner. She was also a very pretty bird, bright yellow below, olive-yellow on the back, no black about the face, and legs and feet blue as the sky, and she was as graceful as she was beautiful.

Repose of manner was unknown to the orchard orioles. One was scarcely ever seen sitting or standing still. The song was given while moving, either flying or hopping about on the tree. If one did pause while it was uttered, the body jerked, and the head turned this way and that, as though he really was too restless to be perfectly quiet for a moment.

The most tempestuous times were when the younger suitor put himself forward and persuaded the fair yellow damsel to show him some slight preference. The venerable lover was not slow to resent this, and to fall like a hurricane upon the pretender, who disappeared like a dead leaf before the blast, and so quickly that he could not be followed—at least by anything less rapid than wings. Once, however, I saw a curious affair between the two suitors which was plainly a war-dance. It followed closely upon one of the usual flurries, conducted with perhaps louder cries and more vehemence than common, and began by both birds alighting on the grass about a foot apart, and so absorbed in each other as to be utterly oblivious of a spectator within ten feet of them on the balcony. No tiger out of the jungle could hold more rage and fury than animated those feathered atoms, bristled up even to the heads, which looked as if covered with velvet caps. They paused an instant, then crouched, jerked their tails, "teetered" and posed in several attitudes, ending each new movement with a solemn bow, perhaps equivalent to a handshake among larger fighters. What one did the other exactly copied, and both seemed to be trying to get one side of the opponent, so as to secure some advantage. To prevent this, each kept his face to the foe, and moved as he moved. Thus they passed down one side, then back, down the other and return, neither able to get the slightest superiority of position. It was extremely grotesque, and was continued several minutes, while I eagerly watched to see what would happen next. What did happen was entirely unexpected, a unique anti-climax, quite worthy of the undignified character of the bird. On a sudden, as by one consent, both flew opposite ways; both alighted in low trees about thirty feet apart, and each one sang a loud joyous song, as of victory!

In this turbulent way life went on for two or three weeks; I could not tell how long, for it was in full progress when I came. There was always a vulgar broil, often a furious encounter, stopping just short of coming to blows, and it seemed really doubtful if the orioles would succeed in settling their matrimonial affairs before summer. The third member of the belligerent party, the demure little object of all this agitation, was meekness and gentleness itself, never aggressive, but always flying before the furious onslaught of her would-be spouse. Why then did she not select her mate and thus end the trouble, which, according to the books, it must do?

Turning away from the more conspicuous males with their endless contests, and watching her closely, I saw that she was trying her best to do so. She plainly preferred the younger and less quarrelsome suitor, and often followed him off, bringing down upon herself in consequence the wrath of the elder, and instant pursuit, which ended in the disappearance of her chosen hero, and a forced endurance of the tyrant's presence, till it appeared that she would have to "marry him to get rid of him," as our plain-spoken grandmothers characterized a similar situation in human affairs.

When these birds could spare time from their own absorbing matters, they were very inquisitive in the affairs of their neighbors. After the mocking-bird babies were out, the orioles often visited them, while the parents were absent, for no reason that I could discover but to see what they were like, and how they got on, for nothing about them was disturbed. If, however, an oriole was found by one of the old mocking-birds perched on the edge of the nest, he was driven away with a piece of mocking-bird mind on the subject of meddlers. Likewise they frequently paid visits to a nuthatch colony at the top of a tall pine-tree. Whether more aggressive among these smaller birds, or not, could not be seen. But the facts were that upon an oriole's disappearing through those heavy pine branches, away above our heads, there instantly arose a great outcry in the querulous nuthatch voice, and the intruder returned to the lower world with some precipitation, while gentle, complaining sounds came from the invaded territory for some time. So, too, in different degree the birds showed interest in me, peering down between the leaves of the tree in which they spent most of their time, and making remarks or expressing opinions, climbing—which they literally did—to the end of a twig, stretching up tall to look over the top and stare at me, or when flying slowly past, hovering a moment just in front of me with perfect fearlessness and earnest attention to my pursuits.

At length the crisis in the oriole matters came, as come it must, and not long after the war-dance that has been described. The season was advanced and nesting time already begun. In fact, it was ended in several families; mocking-birds were about ready to fly, young chipping sparrows peeped from every tuft of grass, baby bluebirds were trying their wings at their doors, the yellow-throated warbler was stuffing her youngsters on the next tree, and the late kingbirds had nearly finished their nests. Whether a pitched battle at last settled the dispute, whether the modest little dame united with her chosen mate against the common enemy, or whether perchance—though this is not likely—the elder bird tired of his useless warfare, will never be known, for the whole matter was settled before we mortals were out of bed, in the magic morning hours when so many interesting things go on in bird and beast life. When I came out, I saw at once that a decision had been reached. The younger bird had won his bride, and with much talk and love-making the happy pair were busying themselves about a building spot. This first day of their honeymoon was not, however, very peaceful; old troubles are not so soon forgotten, and the discarded suitor found it hard to believe that the repulse was final and he really should not have his own way. He frequently made his appearance in the old scenes, making himself agreeable in the usual way; but the newly wedded were now a pair, and when both flung themselves upon him he recognized at last the inevitable, no longer resented it, and left them in peace.

With much talk and discussion the tree that had been the scene of the stormy wooing was selected for the homestead, and the young wife at once set to work upon the foundation, while her spouse in his new rôle of lord and master stood on a higher twig and gave his opinions; much advice, no doubt, and plenty of instruction. I doubt his mastery, however, for I noticed that, though meek, madam had a mind of her own and an orchard oriole's persistence in carrying out her plans. He talked, it is true, blustered and strutted around, but she worked quietly, steadily, and in a business-like way, utterly oblivious of him.

During this day, too, even this first day, not five hours after he had tried to coax the bride away, the elderly suitor came back from some unknown quarter, with a brand-new wife of his own; precipitation worthy of the vulgar house-sparrow of our city streets, which these birds also resemble in their constant broils. That naturally put a complete end to further dispute over sweethearts; but they could not change their nature, and I observed that each young husband had a vast amount of fault to find, much scolding and grumbling. Happily it did not seem to disconcert the little wives; they sang as sweetly, and worked as steadily as though they were used to it, and expected nothing better, which was well for them.

The elder oriole and his mate soon settled in another place, and I saw them no more, but I was sorry to see upon what tree the young pair decided to build, for a kingbird had an unfinished nest in one of the lower branches, and two families so aggressive would make a lively neighborhood no doubt. Hostilities began indeed on the first day. Watching the oriole at her building, I caught the pretty innocent-looking creature stealing material from the kingbird's nest, while her virtuous spouse perched himself on the upper branch of the tree, exactly as if on the watch for returning owners. In a low tone he talked to her as she entered the uncompleted nest, worked busily a moment, then appeared on the edge with a soft white feather, gathered it into a convenient shape, and flew with it in her beak to the upper branch. Twice afterward I saw that performance repeated, and each time it was a white feather taken. On one occasion the kingbird was at home. There was a sharp cry of distress, a bustle, and in a moment Madam Oriole flew off with a feather, while the outraged owner stood on a neighboring branch and uttered two or three plaintive cries. Considering the size and the belligerent nature of the kingbird, I was astonished, but exactly thus it happened.

I greatly wished to stay and see the result, for I had confidence enough in the bravery of the kingbirds to be sure that the end was not yet. Also, I longed to watch the restless pair whose ups and downs I had found so interesting. I should like to see the orchard oriole in the rôle of a father; a terribly fussy one he would be without doubt. Above all, I most desired to see the infant orioles, to know if they begin their quarrels in their narrow cradle, and if their first note is a scold. But the troubles of this courtship had, like the wars of Augustus and Arabella in a three-volume novel, consumed so much time that there was none left for post-nuptial chronicles, and I was obliged to leave them with a neighborhood quarrel on hand which promised full employment for the head of the family while his little mate was sitting.

FLUTTERBUDGET.

O hark to the brown thrush! hear how he sings!
Now he pours the dear pain of his gladness!
What a gush! and from out what golden springs!

What a rage of how sweet madness!

D. A. Wasson.

VIII.

FLUTTERBUDGET.

"Flutterbudget" is the one expressive word that exactly characterizes a certain brown thrush, or thrasher, the subject of a year's study. This bird is perhaps the only restless creature that bears the name of thrush, and he is totally unlike the rest of his family, having neither dignity, composure, nor repose of manner. My brown thrush, however, was exceedingly interesting in his own way, if only as a study of perpetual motion, of the varieties of shape and attitude possible to him, and the fantastic tricks upon wing of which he was capable. One never tired of watching him, for he was erratic in every movement, always inventing some new sort of evolution, or a fresh way of doing the old things, and scarcely a moment at rest. A favorite exercise was flying across the room, planting his feet flatly against the side wall, turning instantly and flying back. This he often did a dozen times in succession. His feet were always "used to save his head" (contrary to our grandmothers' teachings). When he made the usual attempt to fly through the window on his first outing in the room, he went feet first against it, and thus saved himself a bumped head. His movements were abrupt in the extreme, and always so unexpected that he frequently threw the whole feathered family into a panic, apparently without the least intention of doing so. Standing beside the cage of another bird, he would wheel quickly and face the other way, absolutely nothing more, but doing this in a manner so startling that the occupant of the cage scolded roundly. He specially delighted in clambering all over the cage of a goldfinch, acting as if he should tear it in pieces, and greatly annoying the small bird. He often flew up the side of the window casing, as though climbing it like a ladder, his feet touching it now and then; and he did the same on the curtains of coarse net. Again he flew across the room before the three windows, turning to each one in turn, planted his feet squarely on the linen shade, as on the wall above mentioned, and without a pause passed to the end of the room, and touched it with his feet in the same strange way. Often when standing for the moment perfectly still before a window, he suddenly flew up, put both feet in this unbirdlike way against the window-shade, turned and went to his cage. In like manner he came in contact with a cage, the books on the shelves, the back of a chair, or any piece of furniture, taking from that point a new direction. When startled he instantly bounded into the air as though the ground were hot under his feet, and often turned a corner or two before he came down. In the middle of his most lovely song he was quite likely, without the least warning, to make a mad dash somewhere, turn a sharp corner, dive in another direction, and alight on the spot he had left a moment before, and all in so spasmodic a way that every bird was panic-stricken.

The thrasher was exceedingly wary, and nothing was droller than his manner of approaching anything, whether a worm I had thrown on the matting for him, or the bathing-dish. In the case of the worm, the moment he saw his prey— which I selected for its liveliness—he came to a nearer perch, and stood there a few minutes, posturing, shaking his plumage in great excitement, looking at me and then at the tempting object. Very soon he dropped to the floor and started towards the worm in the funniest way; running a few steps, stopping short and turning half round, ready for instant flight, flirting his feathers with a great rustle, turning an anxious eye on me, then on the wriggling attraction, running a step or two, and repeating the performance. In this way he advanced very gradually till near enough to half encircle his prey; or to run and hop sideways as though to describe a circle, turning away at each pause as before, all the time jerking and fluttering in intense agitation, and always keeping an eye on me. Not that he was in the least afraid of me; it was simply his sensational way of doing everything. When he finally came within reach of the worm, he snatched it, and ran as though the enemy were upon him.

His performances before entering the bath were even more amusing. The bathing-dish, a broad, deep plate, stood upon a towel on a table. The bird alighted on the table, and began first to peck the towel, pulling the fringe, working at any loose thread he discovered, and industriously enlarging any small hole he chanced to find. In doing thus he often turned over the edge, when he sprang back as though he had seen a ghost. Recovering from the shock, he circled around the dish with little hops, occasionally giving a gentle peck at the edge of the dish, or a snip at the water with his beak. Thus he waltzed around the bath perhaps forty times, now and then going so far as to jump up on the edge, make a dash at the water, and back off as if it were hot, or to give a hop into the middle of the water and out again so quickly that one could hardly believe he touched it. When, after all this ceremony, he did go in to stay, he made most thorough work, splashing in a frantic way, as though he had but a moment to stay, and in one minute getting more soaked than many birds ever do. After this short dip he dashed out, flew to a perch, and in the maddest way jerked and shook himself dry; pulling his feathers through his beak with a snap, and making a peculiar sound which I can liken only to the rubbing of machinery that needs oil.

The brown thrush was never so violent and eccentric in movement as just after his bath. Allowing himself often but a moment's hasty shake of plumage, he darted furiously across the room, startling every bird, and alighting no one could guess where. Then, after more jerks and rapid shakings, he flung himself as unexpectedly in another direction, while at every fresh turn birds scattered wildly, everywhere, anywhere, out of his way, bringing up in the most unaccustomed places; as, for instance, a dignified bird, who never went to the floor, coming to rest under the bed, or a ground-lover flattened against the side of a cage. All this disturbance seemed to please the thrasher, for he had a spice of mischief in his composition. A never failing diversion was teasing a goldfinch. He began his pranks by entering the cage and hammering on the tray, or digging into the seed in a savage way that sent it flying out in a shower, which result so entertained him that I was forced to close the door when the owner was out. This the thrush resented, and he next took to jumping against the side of the cage, clinging a moment, then bouncing off with so much force that the cage rocked violently. Then he placed himself on the perch by the door, and pounded, and pulled, and jerked, and shook the door, till, if the owner were home, he was nearly wild. Having exhausted that amusement, he jumped on the top and in some way jarred the cage roughly. To protect it I made a cover of paper, but, contrary to my intentions, this afforded the rogue a new pleasure, for he soon found that by tramping over it he could make a great noise, and he quickly learned the trick of tearing the paper into pieces, and uncovering the little fellow, who, by the way, was not in the least afraid, but simply enraged and insulted, and when outside stood and faced his tormentor, blustering and scolding him well.

Tearing paper was always amusing to the brown thrush. I have seen him take his stand near the wall, peck at the paper till he found a weak spot where it would yield and break, then take the torn edge in his bill and deliberately tear it a little. It was "snatching a fearful joy," however, for the noise always startled him. First came a little tear, then a leap one side, another small rent, another panic; and so he went on till he had torn off a large piece which dropped to the floor, while I sat too much interested in the performance to think of saving the paper. (The room and its contents are always secondary to the birds' comfort and pleasure, in my thoughts.) A newspaper on the floor furnished him amusement for hours, picking it to pieces, tearing pictures, from which he always first pecked the faces, dragging the whole about the floor to hear it rattle and to scare himself with. A pile of magazines on a table made a regular playground for him, his plan being to push and pull at the back of one till he got it loose from the rest, and then work at it till it fell to the floor. He never failed to reduce the pile to a disreputable-looking muss.

The bird was as fond of hammering as any woodpecker, on the bottom of his cage, on perches, on the floor, even on his food; and his leaps or bounds without the apparent help of his wings were extraordinary. Not infrequently I have seen him spring into the air just high enough to see me over my desk,—three feet at least,—probably to satisfy himself as to my whereabouts, and drop instantly back to his work or play.

This amusing bird was also intelligent. He understood perfectly well what I wanted when I spoke to him; that is, he had a guilty conscience when in mischief that translated my tone to him. Also he recognized instantly a bird out of place, as, for instance, one on the floor which usually frequented the perches and higher parts of the room; and having taken upon himself the office of regulator, he always went after the bird thus out of his accustomed beat. When I talked to the thrasher, he answered me not only with a rough-breathing sound, a sort of prolonged "ha-a-a," but with his wings as well. Of course this is not uncommon in birds, but none that I have seen use these members so significantly as he did. His way was to lift the wing nearest me, sometimes very slightly, sometimes to a perpendicular position, but only one wing, and only after I made a remark. This exhibition was curious and interesting, and I often prolonged my talk to see the variety he could give to this simple motion. His wings were always expressive, in alighting in a new place, or where he suspected there might be danger or a surprise; the moment his feet touched he lifted one or both wings quite high, dropping them at once.

A more lithe body than that of the brown thrush I have never seen in feathers; he could assume as many attitudes as he had emotions. He often stood on a perch and postured for a long time, as if greatly excited and meditating some mad deed, and I must confess he usually carried out the intention. Not only was he able to put his body into all possible shapes, but he had extraordinary command of his feathers. He could erect them on any one part alone, on the top of the head, the shoulders, the back, or the chin. He often raised the feathers just above the tail, letting that member hang straight down, giving him the appearance of being chopped square off.

The song of this bird is well known and quite celebrated; indeed, in the Southern States he is called the French mocking-bird, as only second to the mocking-bird proper. My bird never sang above a whisper, one may say; that is, he never opened his mouth to let out the sound, though he was extremely fond of singing, indulging in it by the hour. He hardly paused for eating, or flying, or hopping around on the floor, but dropped sweet notes in between the mouthfuls, and kept up the warble through all movements.

As dusk came on the brown thrush began a wonderful series of postures, more peculiar and varied than one would suppose possible to so large and apparently clumsy a bird. Sometimes he stretched up very tall, then instantly crouched as if about to spring; one moment he turned his head downward as though to dive off, then wheeled and faced the other way; now he drew his body out long to a point, head and tail exactly on a level, then head and tail thrust up, making his back the shape of a bow; at one time he threw his head back as though about to turn a back somersault, then scraped his bill, shook himself out, and made the harsh breathing I have spoken off; in another moment he spread his tail like a fan, and instantly closed it again; then turned his head on one side very far, while his tail hung out the other side, and in this odd position jerked himself along by short jumps the whole length of his perch. Between the postures and on every occasion he scraped his bill violently. Next began movements: first he ran down his three perches, across the floor, and hopped to the upper one from the outside, touching his feet to the wires as he went, so rapidly that my eyes could not follow him; then he alighted on the perch with a graceful flop of one wing, sometimes also bowing his head several times, and uttering the breathing sound each time. Again he jumped from the upper perch to one directly under it, and returned the same way by a very peculiar motion: standing on the lower perch, he turned his head over his shoulder, and sprang back and up at the same time, landing in exactly the same position on the perch above, with perfect ease and grace.

Nothing pleased the thrasher more than watching other birds; he observed them closely, especially liking to stand on top of a cage and see the life below,—an agitated life it was apt to be when he was there. Thus he sometimes stood on the goldfinch's cage and noticed every motion with great interest, yet with an indescribably ironical air, as if he said, "My dear sir, is *that* the way you eat?" He showed particular interest in seed-eating birds, apparently not understanding how they could enjoy such food. Though full of bluster and pretense, he was as gentle as any bird in the room, never presumed on his size as the biggest, and, though liking to tease and worry, never really touching one. The smallest only needed to stand and face him to see that it was all bluster and fun.

All this until spring began to stir his blood and tempt him occasionally, after long posturing and many feints, to deliver a gentle dig at a neighbor's ribs. Now, too, he began to show interest in out-of-doors, standing on the window sash and looking out, which is a familiar sign that a bird's time to depart has come. In his case I did not consider it necessary to carry him to the park to liberate him, for I was sure he could take care of the sparrows and protect himself—and so it proved. When he found himself suddenly on a tall tree in the street, and before he recovered from his surprise, those disreputable birds gathered around him to see what he was like. They soon found out; he quickly recovered himself, made a wild dash that scattered them like leaves before the wind, and then planted himself on a branch to await another attempt. But sparrows, though saucy, are knowing, and not one came near him again. They had quite satisfied their curiosity, and after a few moments' waiting the brown thrush went on his way rejoicing.

"O WONDROUS SINGERS."

In the swamp in secluded recesses
A shy and hidden bird is warbling a song.

Sing on! sing on, you gray-brown bird!
Sing from the swamps, the recesses, pour
Your chant from the bushes;
O liquid and free and tender!
O wild and loose to my soul!
O wondrous singer!

Walt Whitman.

IX.

"O WONDROUS SINGERS."

I feel considerable reluctance in approaching the subject of my small thrushes. None but a poet should speak of them—so beautiful, so enchanting in song. Yet I cannot bear to let their lovely lives pass in silence; therefore if they must needs remain unsung, they shall at least be chronicled.

There were two: one the gray-cheeked thrush, the other the veery or Wilson's, and they passed a year in my house, filling it with a marvelous rippling music like the sweet babble of a brook over stones; like the gentle sighing of the wind in pine-trees; like other of nature's enchanting sounds, which I really must borrow a poet's words to characterize:

"O liquid and free and tender!

O wild and loose to my soul!

O wondrous singer."

The gray-cheeked, most charming in every look and motion, uttered his notes in a free sweep or crescendo, which began low, gathered force as he went on, and then gradually died out; all in one long slur, without a defined or staccato note, making a wonderful resemblance to wind sounds, as Emerson expresses it:

"His music was the Southwind's sigh."

The song of the veery was quite different, low, rapid, interspersed with a louder, wild-sounding cry, or, as aptly described by a listener, like the gurgling sounds made by blowing through a tube into soft water, with occasional little explosions. The soft, whispered warble of a brown thrush added a certain under-tone which combined and harmonized both these, forming with them a rhapsody of a rippling, bubbling character impossible to describe, but constantly reminding one of running streams, and gentle water-falls, and coming nearer to "put my woods in song" than any other bird-notes whatever. Neither of the performers opened his mouth, so that the trio was very low, a true whisper-song.

It was somewhat curious that with one exception all the birds in the room through these months sang whisper-songs also, without opening the bill. There were six of them, and every one delighted in singing; the three thrushes, a bluebird, a female orchard oriole, and a Mexican clarin. To the thrushes, music seemed necessary to life; hour after hour they stood on their respective perches across the room, puffed out into balls, "pouring out their souls," and entrancing us not only with their suggestive melody, but with graceful and poetical movements, and a beauty of look and bearing that moved one deeply. During the aria both birds stood motionless, one with wings drooping, and accenting every note, the other with tail slightly jerking for the same purpose.

In character no less than in song the birds differed; bright, active and high-spirited, the gray-cheeked delighted in the freedom of the room, feared nothing, came upon the desk freely, and calmly met one's eyes with his own, brave free soul that he was, while his *vis-à-vis* was timid and shy, could not be induced to leave the shelter of his home though the door stood open all day. He never resented the intrusion of a neighbor, nor disputed the possession of his own dish.

Almost as interesting as his song was a bewitching dance with which the gray-cheeked charmed every one fortunate enough to see him. His chosen hour was the approach of evening, when, with body very erect and head thrown up in ecstasy, he lifted his wings high above his back, fluttering them rapidly with a sound like soft patter of summer rain, while he moved back and forth on his perch with the daintiest of little steps and hops: now up, now down, now across the cage, with gentle noise of feet and wings. No music accompanied it, and none was needed—it was music itself. Not only did he dance away the long hours of twilight, till so dark he could not be seen, but he greeted the dawn in the same way; long before any other bird stirred, before the hideous morning call of the first sparrow in the street, the soft flutter of his wings, the light patter of his feet was heard. In the night also, if gas was lighted, however dimly, dancing began and was continued in the darkness, long after the light was out and every other feather at rest. A sudden light stopped the motion, but revealed the dancer agitated, stirred, with soft dark eyes fixed upon the observer. This dance was not an attempt or indication of a desire to escape, as I am sure for several reasons. I can tell the instant that longing for freedom sets in. It was a fresh sign of the strange, mysterious emotion with which all thrushes greet the rising and setting of the sun.

The singular use of the feet by this bird was very peculiar, and not confined to his dancing hours. While standing on the edge of the bathing-dish, longing, yet dreading to enter the water, on alighting upon an unaccustomed perch, or venturing on to the desk, many times a day he took the little steps, lifting first one, then the other foot very slightly, and bringing it down with a sound without changing his position. It seemed to be an evidence of excitement, as another bird might exhibit by a quivering of the wings. The veery was also a dancer, but in a different way. He fanned his wings violently and moved back and forth across the top of a cage, but always in daylight, and then only on the rare occasions when, by placing his food outside, he was coaxed from his cage.

Bathing was—next to singing—the dear delight of the gray-cheeked's life, yet no bird ever had more misgivings about taking the fatal plunge. His first movement on leaving the cage was to go to the bath, around which he hovered, now this side, now that, one moment on the perch above, the next on the edge of the dish, plainly longing to be in, yet the mere approach of the smallest bird in the room drove him away. Not that he was afraid, he was not in the least a coward; he met everybody and everything with the dignity and bravery of a true thrush. Neither was it that he was disabled when wet, which makes some birds hesitate; he was never at all disordered by his bath, and however long he soaked, or thoroughly he spattered, his plumage remained in place and he was perfectly able to fly at once. It appeared simply that he could not make up his mind to go in. Then too, it soon became apparent that he noticed his reflection in the water. He often stood on the edge after bathing, as well as before, looking intently upon the image. Before the glass he did the same, looking earnestly and in a low tone "uttering his thoughts to the ideal bird which he fancied he saw before him." Indeed, I think this ideal thrush was a great comfort to him.

Once having decided to go into the bath he enjoyed it exceedingly, though in an unusual way, fluttering and splashing vigorously for a moment, then standing motionless up to his body in the water, not shaking or pluming himself, not alarmed, but quietly enjoying the soaking. After several fits of splashing alternated with soaking, he went to a perch and shook and plumed himself nearly dry, and just when one would think he had entirely finished, he returned to the dish, and began again—hesitating on the brink, coquetting with the "ideal thrush" in the water, and in fact doing the whole thing over again.

My bird had a genuine thrush's love of quiet and dislike of a crowd, preferred unfrequented places to alight on, and was quite ingenious in finding them. The ornamental top of a gas-fixture a few inches below the ceiling, which was cup-shaped and nearly hid him, was a favorite place. So was also the loose edge of a hanging cardboard map which, having been long rolled, hung out from the wall like a half-open scroll. This he liked best, for no other bird ever approached it, and here he passed much time swinging, as if he enjoyed the motion which he plainly made efforts to keep up. His plan was to fly across the room and alight suddenly upon it, when, of course it swayed up and down with his weight. The moment it came to a rest, he flew around the room in a wide circle and came down again heavily, holding on with all his might, and keeping his balance with wings and tail. He enjoyed it so well that he often swung for a long time.

Later he found another snug retreat where no bird ever intruded. He discovered it in this way: one day, on being suddenly startled by an erratic dash around the room of the brown thrush, which scattered the smaller birds like leaves before the wind, he brought up under the bed on the floor. The larger bird had evidently marked the place of his retreat, for he followed him, and in his mad way rushed under when the gray-cheeked disappeared. The bedstead was a light iron one, high from the floor, so that all this was plainly seen. No one being in sight, the brown thrush came out and turned to his regular business of stirring up the household while the little thrush was not to be seen, and perfect silence seemed to indicate that he was not there at all. After some search, aided by an indiscreet movement on his part, he was found perched on the framework, between the mattress and the wall. This narrow retreat, apparently discovered by accident, soon became a favorite retiring place when he did not care for society.

This interesting bird, with all his dignity, had a playful disposition. Nothing pleased him better than rattling and tearing to bits a newspaper or the paper strips over a row of books, although he had to stand on the latter while he worked at it; and notwithstanding it not only rustled, but disturbed his footing as well, he was never discouraged. A more violent jerk than usual sometimes startled him so that he bounded six or eight inches into the air in his surprise, but he instantly returned to the play and never rested till he had picked holes, torn pieces out, and reduced it to a complete wreck.

All through the long winter this charming thrush, with his two neighbors, delighted the house with his peculiar and matchless music, and endeared himself by his gentle and lovely disposition. No harsh sound was ever heard from him, there was no intrusion upon the rights of others, and no vulgar quarrels disturbed his serene soul. But as spring began to stir his blood he changed a little; he grew somewhat belligerent, refused to let any one alight in his chosen places, and even drove others away from his side of the room. Now, too, he added to his already melting song an indescribable trill, something so spiritual, so charged with the wildness of the woods, that no words—even of a poet—can do it justice. Now, too, he began to turn longing glances out of the window, and evidently his heart was no longer with us. So, on the first perfect day in May he was taken to a secluded nook in a park and his door set open. His first flight was to a low tree, twenty feet from the silent spectator, who waited, anxious to see if his year's captivity had unfitted him for freedom.

Perching on the lowest branch, the thrush instantly crouched in an attitude of surprise and readiness for anything, which was common with him, his bill pointed up at an angle of forty-five degrees, head sunk in the shoulders, and tail standing out stiffly, thus forming a perfectly straight line from the point of his beak to the tip of his tail. There he stood, perfectly motionless, apparently not moving so much as an eyelid for twenty minutes, trying to realize what had happened to him and in the patient, deliberate manner of a thrush to adjust himself to his new conditions. In the nook were silence and delicious odors of the woods; from a thick shrub on one side came the sweet erratic song of a cat-bird, and at a little distance the rich organ-tones of the wood-thrush. All these entered the soul of the emancipated bird; he listened, he looked, and at last he spoke, a low, soft, "wee-o." That broke the spell, he drew himself up, hopped about the tree, flew to a shrub, all the time posturing and jerking wings and tail in extreme excitement and no doubt happiness to the tips of his toes. At last he dropped to the ground and fell to digging and reveling in the soft loose earth with enthusiasm. The loving friend looking on was relieved; this was what she had waited for, to be assured that he knew where to look for supplies, and though she left his familiar dish full of food where he could see it in case of accident, she came away feeling that he had not been incapacitated for a free life by his months with her.

One more glimpse of him made it clear also that he could fly as well as his wild neighbors, and removed the last anxiety about him. A wood-thrush, after noticing the stranger for some minutes, finally braved the human presence and made a rush for the little fellow about half his size. Whether war or welcome moved him was not evident, for away they flew across the nook, not more than a foot apart, now sweeping low over the grass, then mounting higher to pass over the shrubs that defined it. A hundred feet or more the chase continued, and then the smaller bird dropped into a low bush, and the larger one passed on.

Then lonely, with empty cage and a happy heart-ache, his friend turned away and left the beautiful bird to his fate, assured that he was well able to supply his needs and to protect himself—in a word, to be free.

A BIRD OF AFFAIRS.

But now the sun is rising calm and bright;
The jay makes answer as the magpie chatters,
And all the air is filled with pleasant sound of waters,
All things that love the sun are out of doors.
Wordsworth.

X.

A BIRD OF AFFAIRS.

One of the most interesting birds I have studied was a blue-jay; I may say is, for he stands at this moment not six feet from me, his whole mind intent upon the business of driving small corks through a hole which they snugly fit. He takes the cork, as he does everything, lengthwise, and turns it about till he gets the smaller end outside; then pushes it into the hole and pounds it, delivering straight and rapid strokes with his iron beak, till it is not only driven up to the head, but, since he has found out that he can do so, till it drops out on the other side, when, after an interested glance to see where it has fallen, he instantly goes to the floor for another, and repeats the performance. Hammering, indeed, is one of his chief pleasures, and no woodpecker, whose special mission it is supposed to be, can excel him; in excitement, in anger, when suffering from *ennui* or from embarrassment, he always resorts to that exercise to relieve his feelings. I have thought sometimes he did it to hear the noise and to amuse himself, in which case it might be called drumming.

Not only does my bird occupy himself with corks, but with perches and the woodwork of his cage, with so great success that the former have to be frequently renewed, and the latter looks as though rats had nibbled it. The deliberate way in which he goes to work to destroy his cage is amusing, lifting the end of a perch and quietly throwing it to the floor, or pounding and splitting off a big splinter of the soft pine and carefully hiding it. To give him liberty, as I have, is simply to enlarge the field of his labors, and furnish him congenial employment from morning to night, the happiest and busiest member of the household. He tries everything: the covers of cardboard boxes, always choosing the spot that is weakest at the corner, and pounding till it is ruined; the cane seats of chairs, which he selects with equal judgment, and never leaves till he has effected a breach; a delicate work-basket, at which he labors with enthusiasm, driving his pickaxe bill into it and cutting a big hole. It is most curious to see him set himself to pick a hole, for instance, in a close-woven rattan chair, or a firm piece of matting stretched upon the floor. Selecting, by some esoteric wisdom, the most vulnerable spot, he pushes and pounds and pokes till he gets the tip of his beak under a strand, and then pulls and jerks and twists till he draws it out of its place. After this the task is easy, and he spends hours over it, ending with a hole in the matting three or four inches in diameter; for he is never discouraged, and his persistence of purpose is marvelous. Books are a special object of his attentions; not only does he peck the backs as they stand on the shelves, till he can insert his beak and tear off a bit, but if he finds one lying down he thrusts the same useful instrument into the edge, slightly open so as to enclose two or three leaves, and then, with a dexterous twist of the head, jerks out a neat little three-cornered piece. Thus he goes on, and after a short absence from the room I have found a great litter of white bits, and my big dictionary curiously scalloped on the edges. He is able to pound up as well as down, crouching, turning his head back, and delivering tremendous blows on the very spot he wishes, and so accurately that he easily cuts a thread, holding its strands under one toe.

But hammering, though a great pleasure, is not his dearest delight. The thing for which, apparently, he came into the world is to put small objects out of sight,—bury them, in fact. No doubt the business for which Nature fitted him, and which in freedom he would follow with enthusiasm, is the planting of trees; to his industry we probably owe many an oak and nut tree springing up in odd places. In captivity, poor soul, he does the best he can to fulfill his destiny. When he has more of any special dainty than he can eat at the moment, as meat, or bread and milk, he hides it at the back of his tray, or in the hole already spoken of in connection with the corks; and when outside, nothing can be droller than the air of concern with which he goes around the floor, picking up any small thing he finds, left purposely for him, a burnt match, a small key, stray pins, or a marble, and seeks the very best and most secluded spot in the room in which to hide it. A pin he takes lengthwise in his mouth, which he closes as though he had swallowed it, as at first I feared he had. He has no doubt about the best place for that; he long ago decided that between the leaves of a book is safest. So he proceeds at once to find a convenient volume, and thrusts the pin far in out of sight. A match gives him the most trouble. He tries the cracks under the grooves in the moulding of the doors, the base board, between the matting and the wall, or under a rocker; in each place he puts it carefully, and pounds it in, then hops off, giving me one of the

"sidelong glances wise

Wherewith the jay hints tragedies,"

attempting to look unconcerned, as if he had not been doing anything. But if he sees that he is observed, or the match is too plainly in sight, he removes it and begins again, running and hopping around on the floor with the most solemn, business-like air, as though he had the affairs of nations on his shoulders, the match thrust nearly its whole length into his mouth. The place usually decided upon is an opening between the breadths of matting. It is amusing when he chances to get hold of a box of matches, accidentally left open, for he feels the necessity and importance of disposing of each one, and is busy and industrious in proportion to the task before him. It is not so pleasing, however, when, in his hammering, he sets one off, as he often does; for they are "parlor matches," and light with a small explosion, which frightens him half out of his wits, and me as well, lest he set the house afire. The business of safely and securely secreting one match will frequently occupy him half an hour. He finds the oddest hiding-places, as in a caster between the wheel and its frame; up inside the seat of a stuffed chair, to reach which he flies up on to the webbing and goes in among the springs; in the side of my slipper while on my foot; in the loop of a bow; in the plaits of a ruffle; under a pillow. Often when I get up, a shower of the jay's treasures falls from various hiding-places about my dress,—nails, matches, shoe-buttons, and others; and I am never sure that I shall not find soft, milk-soaked bread in my slipper. But the latest discovered and most annoying of his receptacles is in my hair. He delights in standing on the high back of my rocking-chair, or on my shoulder, and he soon discovered several desirable hiding-places conveniently near, such as my ear, and under the loosely dressed hair. I did not object to his using these, but when he attempted to tuck away some choice thing between my lips I rebelled. I never expect to find a keyhole that he can reach, free from bread crumbs, and the openings of my waste-basket are usually decorated with objects half driven in.

The jay shows unbounded interest in everything. Every sound and every fresh sight arouses him instantly; his crest comes up, his feathers fluff out, and he is on tiptoe to see what will come next. He is remarkably discriminating among people, and takes violent likes and dislikes on the instant. Some persons, without any reason that I can discover, he salutes on their first appearance with an indescribable cry, like "obble! obble! obble!" At others he squawks madly. On one occasion he took an intense dislike to a lady, of whom birds generally are very fond, and he made a peculiar display of rage, squawking and screaming at her, raising his crest, stamping, snapping his beak, giving vicious digs at the side of the cage, as though he would eat her if he could reach her. And although he often saw her, and she tried her best to win him, he always showed the same spirit, going so far, when out of his cage, as to show fight, fly up at her, peck her savagely, and chase her to the door when she left. Again, a lady came in with her baby, and he at once singled out the infant as his enemy, fixing a very wicked glance on it, but in perfect silence. He jumped back and forth as if mad to get out, and sat with open mouth, panting as if exhausted, with eyes immovably turned to the baby. He would not pay the slightest attention to any one else, nor answer me when I spoke, which was very unusual, till they left the room, when the moment the door closed behind them he began rapidly, as if to make up for lost time. Some visitors whom he fancies, he receives in silence, but with slightly quivering wings; only the very few he loves best are greeted with a low, sweet, and very peculiar chatter, which he keeps up as long as he is talked to.

Investigating everything in the room is one of my bird's greatest pleasures, and most attractive of all he finds the drawer of my desk, on the edge of which he stands, delighted and bewildered by the variety before him. Great would be the havoc if I were not there; and the curious thing about it is that he will pull things over carelessly, with one eye on me, to see if I object. If, on touching some particular thing, he sees that I do not approve,—and he recognizes my sentiment as quickly as a bright child would,—that thing, and that only, he will have. At once he snatches it and flies away across the room, and I may chase him in vain. He regards it as a frolic got up for his amusement, and no child ever equaled him in dodging; he cannot be driven, and if cornered he uses his wings. I simply put my wits against his, follow him about till he has to drop his load to breathe, when a sudden start sends him off, and I secure it. If I cover up anything, he knows at once it is some forbidden treasure, and devotes all his energy and cunning, which are great, to uncovering and possessing himself of it. He opens any box by delivering sharp blows under the edge of the cover, and hides my postage stamps in books and magazines. He hops around the floor in a heavy way, as often sideways as straight, and holds his toes as close together as though he had worn tight boots all his life. If startled, he bounds up into the air in the oddest way, a foot or two, or even more, generally turning half round, and coming down with his head the other way. If much alarmed he will bounce up in this way half a dozen times in quick succession, and should he happen to be on a table at the time, he usually ends by landing on the floor. His alighting after any flight is most singular: he comes to the floor in a crouching position, legs sprawled, body horizontal and nearly touching the matting, looking like a bird gone mad; then instantly springs up six or eight inches, half turns, and stands upright, crest erect, and looking excited, almost frightened. If much disturbed he comes down with wings half open, tail held up, and every feather awry, as if he were out in a gale, uttering at the same time a loud squawk. He is a most expert catcher, not only seizing without fail a canary seed thrown to him, but even fluttering bits of falling paper, the hardest of all things to catch.

The blue-jay is a bird of opinions about most things, and able to express himself quite clearly; as, for example, when he found himself under a chair without rounds, on which he likes to perch, he stood and looked around on every side, and made a low, complaining cry, plainly a protest against so unnatural a chair; and again, when he scolded at the rain that came in sudden gusts against the window, or charged furiously at the crack under a door when he heard sweeping outside. In general he is very quiet when one is in the room, but the moment the door closes behind the last person his voice is heard,—whistling exactly like a boy, calling, squawking, and occasionally uttering a sweet, though not loud song, which is varied by a sound like rubbing a cork against glass. The most quiet approach silences him. When under strong emotion he may squawk or scream before spectators, but he never whistles or sings when he knows any one is in the room. When out of his sight and so long silent that he has forgotten me, I have now and then heard the song.

The funniest thing this knowing fellow does is to stamp his feet, and it is a genuine expression of impatience or displeasure. When I take something away from him or he thinks I mean to do so, or refuse him something he wants, he stands still and jerks his feet in such a way that they stamp with a loud sound, as if they were of iron. It is very droll. In serious anger, he adds to this, bowing and curtsying by bending the legs, snapping the bill, pecking, and jumping up with the body without lifting the feet.

It may be that the jay in freedom disturbs other birds, as has been affirmed, but among a number smaller than himself my bird has never once shown the least hostility. He is interested in their doings, but the only unpleasant thing he has done is to shriek and scream to stop their singing. In spite of his natural boldness, always facing the enemy, always ready to fight, and never running from danger nor allowing himself to be driven anywhere, when he is not quite well he is a timid bird. In moulting, this spring, my jay lost his entire tail, and was extremely awkward in getting about, almost helpless, in fact; and at that time he was afraid to hop to the floor, and refused to come out of the cage. (I should have said, by the way, that he feared hurting himself; he was quite as spirited as ever, as ready to show fight.) To get him out of the door I offered him the greatest inducements, with the cage on the floor, so that he could not fall far. He would stand on the lowest perch, three inches from the floor, look at the meat or whatever treasure I placed in the open doorway, and cry a faint, low, jay-baby cry, yet not dare descend, though plainly aching with desire to get the object so nearly within his reach. Even since he is entirely recovered and the possessor of a beautiful long tail, he dreads the one little step and has to be coaxed out and in his cage every day, as we coax a startled child.

Nothing ever interested the jay more than a piano, though he is fond of any music. The first time he heard one he quickly hopped across to the player, pulled at the hem of her dress, flew up to her lap, then her arm, and mounted to her shoulder, where he stood some time, looking and listening, turning his head this way and that, raising his crest, jerking his body, and in every way showing intense excitement. Finally he took his last step, to the top of her head, where he was more pleased to be than the player was to have him. She put him down; and the next time he tried a different way, mounted to the keys, and thence to the cover, crouching and peering under the lid to see where the sounds came from. Satisfied about this, he returned to her head, which he evidently considered the best post of observation. Every time she played she received the devoted attentions of the bird, and he could not be kept away.

My blue-jay is now a beautiful creature, in perfect plumage, with breast and back plumes so long that often in repose, just after he has dressed them, the violet blue of the back meets the light drab of his breast, on the side, covering his wings completely, and making a lovely picture. All through the spring excitement, when the other birds, one after another, grew uneasy, belligerent, or unhappy, and one after another were returned to freedom, he never showed a moment's uneasiness, an instant's desire to be free, but scrupulously attended to his own regular business, which is to pound and pull and peck to pieces my furniture, and especially to destroy my books.

As these last words are written, just at dusk, the dear, troublesome rogue comes down to the corner of his cage nearest to me, and as if he understood that I had said something about him begins to talk and remonstrate in a low, loving tone. I do feel reproached, and I must unsay it. His business, his manifest destiny, is to hammer and peck the shells of nuts, and to hide them away where they will grow; and if cruel man confines him in a house, he must exercise his untiring energy, his demon of work, in what he finds there,—and who can blame him, or find fault? Not I, certainly.

In behalf of this bird against whom the pen of nearly every writer is lifted, let me quote from one of our early and most careful observers, William Bartram: "The jay is one of the most useful agents in the economy of nature for disseminating forest trees and other ruciferous and hard-seeded vegetables on which they feed. These birds alone are capable in a few years' time to replant all the cleared lands." Thoreau, who was perhaps the closest of our modern students of nature, cites this passage and emphatically affirms its justice.

THE BLUE-JAY AGAIN.

As for birds, I do not believe there is one of them but does more good than harm; and of how many featherless bipeds can this be said?

Lowell.

XI.

THE BLUE-JAY AGAIN.

The blue-jay came out of the egg with his mind made up. He always knew exactly what he wanted, and never doubted that he knew how to get it. I wrote of this bird some time ago, but he was then a comparatively new acquaintance. He lived with us many months after that, and became much more familiar; for besides being slow to feel thoroughly at home, he was very young, and he grew in wisdom with age. So I have more to say of him.

Human society was necessary to the jay; he cared for the other birds of the room only as objects on which to play tricks for his own amusement. He was peculiar, too, in never liking more than one friend at a time, and was very decided in his opinions of people, having a distinctly different reception for each one of the household, as well as for strangers. His mistress was always his prime favorite; and although during my absence from home he adopted some one temporarily in my place, he was never so affectionate to that one as to me, and the instant I returned resumed his old relations to each of us.

To his best beloved this bird never squawked or whistled; on the contrary, he talked in low, sweet tones, hardly more than a murmur, slightly lifting and quivering his wings, sidling as near as he could get, and if I put my face down to him touching my cheek or lips gently with his beak, in little taps, like kisses. Any one else in that position would receive a violent peck. Sometimes, when I was busy, and therefore silent a long time, and the jay was in his cage, where I was obliged to put him in order to work at all, he stood perfectly quiet and motionless an hour at a time, moving only when he was hungry, and apparently watching me every instant,—a performance very uncommon in a bird, who usually has some interests of his own, however fond he may be of a person. The moment I spoke to him his whole manner changed. He came at once as near as he could, about four feet from me, and began to talk, holding his tail on one side, and both wings spread to their fullest extent and parallel with his back. In this attitude he hopped up and down his three perches, always as near my side as possible, and evidently in great excitement. If during this exhibition any one came in, his wings instantly dropped, though he did not stop talking to me. This action of the wings showed extreme affection, and must not be profaned by common eyes. When I came close and replied to him, his agitation was almost painful to see,—such loving tones, such gentle kisses, such struggles to express himself. Not only did he insist on sharing his dainties with me, offering me mocking-bird food or bread and milk in the most loving way, but he wished to share mine; ice-cream he delighted in, cake he was as fond of as any child, and

67

candy he always begged for, though instead of eating it he hid it somewhere about the room,—under my pillow, or between the leaves of a book, all sticky as it was from his mouth.

Second in the blue-jay's affection was a lady to whom at first he took a great dislike. She tried her best to win him, talking to him, treating him to various tidbits, and offering him the hospitality of her room,—separated from the bird-room by a passage,—and above all dancing with him. These attentions in time secured her a warm place in his regards, though his treatment of her was very different from that reserved for me. He was always gentle with me, while in her society he exhibited all his noisy accomplishments,—squawked, whistled and screamed, stamped his feet, and jounced (the only word to describe a certain raising and violent dropping of the body without lifting the feet). He ran after her when she left the room; he pecked her hand, and flew up at her face. Gradually, as he grew to like her better, the more violent demonstrations ceased; but he was always boisterous with her, generally expected a half-fight, half-frolic, and I must say never failed to enjoy it greatly.

The dance spoken of was droll. His chosen place for this indulgence was the back of a tall chair. His friend stood before this, whistled, bowed, and moved her head up and down as if dancing; and he on his perch did the same, jumping up and down in a similar way, answering her whistle for whistle, moving his feet, sliding from one side to the other, curtsying, lowering the body and flattening the head feathers, then rising, stamping his feet, and drooping his wings. This he kept up as long as she played second to him.

When this playfellow went away, the jay missed his dances and frolics. He flew into her empty room, perched on the back of the rocking-chair, where he had been wont to stand and pull her hair, and began a peculiar cry. Again and again he repeated it, louder and louder each time, till it ended in a squawk, impatient and angry, as much as to say, "Why don't you answer?" After a while he began to whistle the notes she used to imitate; finding that this brought no response, he returned to the cry; and when at last he had exhausted all his resources, he came back to my desk and consoled himself by talking to me.

A young lady in the family he greeted by flying at her, alighting on her chair-back, clawing her neck, and squawking; and before a youth who often teased him he trailed his wings on the floor, tail spread and dragging also, uttering a curious "obble! obble!" something like the cry of a turkey. The head of the household he met with stamping of the feet, and no sound; while at a maid who came in to sweep he always flew furiously, aiming for her head, and invariably frightening her half out of her wits.

The jay was extremely wary about anything like a trap, and being always on the lookout for one, he sometimes, like bigger persons, fooled himself badly. Finding him fond of standing on a set of turning bookshelves, I thought to please him by arranging over it a convenient resting-place. He watched me with great interest, but, when I had finished, declined to use the perch, though ordinarily nothing could keep him from trying every new thing. I put a bait upon it in the shape of bits of gum-drops, a favorite delicacy; but he plainly saw that I wanted him to go to it, and in the face of the fact that I had heretofore tried to keep him off the papers and magazines lying there, he decided that it was suspicious. He flew so as almost to touch the stick, and hovered before it to snatch off the candy placed there; but alight on it he would not, and did not, though I kept it in place a week.

In many ways this bird was wise; he knew exactly where to deliver his blows to effect what he desired. A cage-door being fastened with fine wire, he never wasted a stroke upon the door, but gave telling blows directly upon the wire. A rubber band was looped about a rod for him to play with, in the expectation that he would pull on it and make sport; but he disappointed us all by hammering at the loop, until he loosened it and easily pulled it off. Again it was tied on with strong linen thread; he turned his whole attention to the knot of the latter, till it yielded and was disposed of also.

Dear as was this bird, he was a more than usually troublesome pet. My desk became his favorite playground, and havoc indeed he made with the things upon it; snatching and running off with paper, pen, or any small object, destroying boxes and injuring books. Finally, in self-defense, I adopted the plan of laying over it every morning a woolen cloth, which must be lifted every time anything was taken from the desk. This arrangement did not please my small friend in blue, and he took pains to express his displeasure in the most emphatic way. He came down upon the cover, tramped all over it, and sought small holes in it through which to thrust his bill. One day he was busily engaged in hammering a book through an opening, and to cure him of the trick I slipped my hand under, caught his beak between two fingers, and held it a moment. This amazed but did not alarm the bird; on the contrary, he plainly decided to persevere till he found out the secret. He pecked the mounds made by my fingers; he stooped and looked into the hole, and then probed again. This time I held him longer, so that he had to struggle and beat his wings to get away, and then he walked off indignantly. Still he was not satisfied about that mystery, and in a moment he was back again, trying in new ways to penetrate it. I was tired before he was. He was baffled only temporarily; he soon learned to draw up the fabric, hold the slack under one foot while he pulled it still further, and thus soon reach anything he desired.

The blue-jay always pried into packages by pecking a hole in the wrapper and examining the contents through that; and boxes he opened by delivering upward blows under the edge of the cover. The waste-basket he nearly emptied from the outside by dragging papers through the openings in the weaving. Seeing two or three unmounted photographs put into a book, he went speedily for that volume, thrust his beak into the slight opening made by the pictures, and pulled them out, flying at once across the room with one in his mouth. It was secured and put back, and the book held down by a heavy weight; but he found the place at once, and repeated the naughtiness. The book had to be completely covered up before the photographs were safe.

After the blue-jay had put on a new suit of feathers he flew with great ease, and selected for a retreat the top of a door into the passageway mentioned, which usually stood open. It was not long before his curiosity was roused to know what was outside the door that so often swallowed up his friends,—that into the hall. He resolved to find out, and to that end, when stationed on the elevated perch of his choice, held himself in readiness, upon the exit of any one, to fly out. He did not wish to get away; he merely took a turn in the hall, and came back; and once, when accidentally left in that unfamiliar place, he stayed in the bath-room, with window wide open, for half an hour before he was found. He became so expert in flying out of the door that it was a difficult matter to pass through without his company; we had to train ourselves in sleight-of-hand to outwit him. There were two ways of getting the better of him; mere suddenness was of no use,—he was much quicker than we were. One way was to go to the room on the other side of the passage, where he was sure to follow, and before he fairly settled there, to dodge back and shut the door,—a proceeding so unexpected that he never learned to allow for it. The other way was to go to the hall-door as if intending to open it; instantly the bird swooped down, ready to slip out also, but finding the way closed, swept around the room and alighted somewhere. This was the second to open the door and step out, for he always paused a moment before flying again.

The only notice the jay ever took of the birds, as said above, was to tease them, or put them in a flutter; as society he plainly despised them. They soon learned to regard him as a sort of infernal machine, liable at any moment to explode; and they were fully justified, for he was fond of surprising them by unexpectedly flying around the room, tail spread, feathers rustling, squawking madly in a loud voice. He usually managed in his career to sweep close over the head of every bird, of course frightening them off their perches, and thus to put the whole room into a panic. They took refuge anywhere,—under the bed, behind the chairs, against the wires, and on the floor,—while the mischief-maker circled around, filling the air with shrieks, then suddenly dropped to the round of a chair and calmly dressed his feathers, as if he had merely been exercising his wings.

Poor little fellow! he was hardly more than a baby, and not very brave. A big grasshopper which once got into the room afforded him great excitement and the spectators much amusement. He saw it before his cage was opened, and as soon as he came out he went after it. The insect hopped up three feet, and so startled the bird that he jumped almost as high. When it alighted he picked it up, but seeming not to know what to do with it, soon dropped it. Again it hopped, and again the jay repeated his bound; and this performance went on for some minutes, one of the drollest of sights,—his cautious approach, the spring of the insect, and his instant copy of the same, as if in emulation. After being picked up several times the grasshopper was disabled; then when the bird came near, it lifted its wings, plainly to scare its persecutor; it did awe him. Meanwhile an orchard oriole had been eagerly looking on, and on one occasion that the grasshopper was dropped he pounced upon it and carried it off to a chair, where he proceeded to eat it, though it was so big as to be almost unmanageable. The jay did not like being deprived of his plaything. He ran after the thief, and stood on the floor, uttering a low cry while watching the operation. In the oriole's moving the clumsy insect fell to the floor, when the jay snatched it; and it was evident that he had got a new idea about its use, for he carried it under a chair and demolished it completely,—not even a wing remained.

More disturbing to the jay, strange as it may seem, was a tree. It was really touching to see a bird afraid of this, but the poor youngster had been taken from the nest to a house. A Christmas tree was brought into the bird-room to please the residents there, when, to our amazement, the jay went into a wild fright, flew madly around near the ceiling, squawking, and making the other birds think something terrible had happened. He flew till he was breathless, and was evidently very much distressed. For three or four days he was equally alarmed the moment he caught sight of it in the morning and whenever I moved it an inch, though the other birds liked it and were on it half the time. When he did get used to it he did not go upon it, but to the standard below, where he could pick the needle-like leaves and carry them off to hide about the room.

The blue-jay took his bath in an original way as he did everything else. First, he stood beside the wide, shallow dish, looked at it, then at me and all around the room, one wing drooping and the other laid jauntily over the back, while he talked in a low tone, as if he said, "If anybody is going to object, now is the time." No one ventured to dispute his right, and suddenly he plumped into the middle, neither alighting on the edge nor testing the water. Then there was a lively frolic, with tail spread, crest raised, wings beating, and the water flying several feet around. He was a very beautiful bird when in perfect-plumage. There were six distinct shades of blue, besides rich velvety black, snowy white, delicate dove color, and blue-gray. He is too well known to need description, but a jay is not often so closely seen when alive and in perfection of plumage. This bird had a charming way of folding his wings that hid all the plain blue-gray. When held thus and laid together over the back, there were displayed first the beautiful tail, with broad white edges to the feathers; above it the wings looking like a square cut mantle, of the same colors; above this a deep pointed shoulder cape, of rich violet blue, the feathers fluffed up loosely; and at the top of all, his exquisite crest.

VIRGINIA'S WOOING.

For who the pleasure of the spring shall tell,
When on the leafless stalk the brown buds swell,
When the grass brightens and the days grow long,
And little birds break out in rippling song.
Celia Thaxter.

XII.

VIRGINIA'S WOOING.

You must know in the beginning that Virginia wore feathers. But she had as many trials with her suitors as though she dressed in silks, and she displayed so much of what we call "human nature" that her story is as interesting as that of half the Ethels and Marguerites of the romances.

She came of a good old family, the Cardinals, and, belonging to the Virginia branch, was called properly Virginia Cardinal, or, in scientific, fashion, *Cardinalis Virginianus*. She was a beauty, too. It is well known that the cardinal himself has a full suit of the most brilliant red, but it is not so familiar a fact that the dames of the tribe are more modest and wear the family colors simply as linings and in subdued tints: rich rose-colored wing-facings, light coral-hued beak, delicate pink crest, all toned down by the soft olive brown of the breast and back, over which is everywhere a lovely suggestion of red.

The home of Virginia, when she came to the bird-room, was a large cage by the window; that of the cardinal being next to it, equally commodious, but a little farther from the light. This personage, her first admirer, made the mistake that larger suitors sometimes fall into, with equally disastrous results,—he "took things for granted." Between the cages was a door, but, to try the temper of the birds, it was at first closed. The cardinal was evidently pleased with his lovely neighbor; he went as near to her as he could get, and uttered some low remarks, to which she listened, but did not reply. Later, when a meal-worm was given to him, he did not eat it, but held it in his beak, hopped over to her side, tried to get through the wires, and plainly thought of offering it to her. His disposition appearing so friendly, a human hand interposed and opened the door. Instantly he went into her cage, and apparently thinking better of the intended offering he ate it himself, and proceeded to investigate her food-dishes and try the seed, then hopped back and forth between the two cages, and at last selected the perch he preferred and took possession. He paid no attention to her in the way of recognizing her ownership, which he would naturally do to another bird; he assumed that whatever belonged to the cardinal family belonged to him; perhaps he even thought she went with the house,—it certainly looked as though he did.

But the little dame had a mind of her own. On his first intrusion she vacated her home and passed into his. When he appeared in his cage she quietly hopped back; on his return she changed cages with equal alacrity; when he settled himself on her perch, she was quite contented on his. There was no dispute, no warfare; she simply said, in manner, "All right, my friend, select your abode, and I'll take the other. I'm satisfied with either, but I intend to have it to myself." After awhile it seemed to strike his lordship that she avoided him, and he resolved to settle that matter; here making his second mistake, in trying to force instead of to win. He entered the cage where she sat quietly, and flew at her. She dodged him and took refuge in the other apartment; he followed; and thus they rushed back and forth several times, till she stopped for breath on a lower perch, while he was on an upper one in the same cage. Then he leaned far over and fixed his eyes on her, crest raised to its greatest height, wings held slightly out, and addressed her in a very low but distinct song, which resembled the syllables "cur-dle-e! cur-dle-e! cr-r-r"; the latter sounding almost like a cat's purr. After singing this several times, and being slighted by her leaving the cage, he laid his crest flat down, muttered something so low that it could not be noted, and looked very much put out. Soon, however, he shook his feathers violently, flung himself at her, and she dodged, as before. When both happened to be for a moment in their own cages, the door was suddenly closed between, and each had his own, as at first. Madam was delighted, but the cardinal resented it; he tried to remove the obnoxious barrier, pecked at it, shook it, and could not be reconciled. He grew hungry and was obliged to eat, but between every two seeds he returned to struggle with the bars that kept him from her. Meanwhile Virginia had apparently forgotten all about him, eating and making her toilet for the night, as cheerful as usual.

The next morning, the outside doors of the two cages were opened, and both birds at once came out into the room. The cardinal, not yet over his tiff of the evening before, took wing for the trees outside the windows, and brought up, of course, against the glass. He was greatly disappointed. He alighted on top of the lower sash, tested, examined, and tried to solve the mystery. Virginia, too, tried to go through the pane, but learned in one lesson that it was useless. She did not care much about it any way, for she was perfectly contented inside. She went around the room, hovering slowly under the ceiling, which is always of interest to birds, and then set herself to work in a most systematic manner to find out all about the new world she was in. She examined the outside perches and tried each one; she explored the bathing table, flirted out a little water from the dishes, and at last thought it time to make acquaintance with her neighbors.

She began with the robin, and flew to his roof. The robin was not pleased, snapped at her, opened his mouth, uttered a queer low robin-cry, "seep," and pecked at her feet, while she stood quietly looking down at the show from above, as much interested as though it were arranged to amuse her. At length she began to make the more formal visit. She dropped to the door-perch and approached the entrance. The inhospitable owner met her there, not to welcome and invite her in, but to warn her out! He lowered his head, opened his beak, and bowed to her, looking very wicked indeed. It was plain that he was "not receiving" that morning. But Virginia had come to call, and call she would. Nothing daunted by his coolness, she hopped in. The robin was amazed; then declared war in his peculiar way,—first a hop of six inches, with wings spread, then a savage clatter of the bill. His guest met this demonstration quite calmly. She lowered her head, to defend herself if necessary, but made no other movement. Her calmness filled the robin with horror; he fled the cage. Then she went all over it, and satisfied herself that it was much like her own, only the food-dish was filled with some uneatable black stuff, instead of the vegetarian food she preferred. She soon departed.

Meanwhile the cardinal was wasting his time over the window problem, touching the glass with his beak, flying up a few inches before it, gently tapping the pane as he went. It was two or three days before he made up his mind he could not get through. After that he was as indifferent to the outside as any bird in the room, and turned his attention once more to Virginia. Whenever they were in their cages, with the door open between, he assumed the lord-and-mastership of the two; he drove her away from her own food-cups, usurped her perch and her cage, and made himself disagreeable generally. Finally, one day when she was sitting quietly on the upper perch of his deserted cage, he came into the same cage, and, resting on the low perch close to the door, his tail hanging outside, began a low call, a curious sort of "e-up," with a jerk on the second syllable. Though a common enough sound for a cardinal, this plainly meant more than was apparent to human spectators. Virginia at once grew uneasy, hopped across the upper perches, and when her nervousness became too great dashed down past him, though he was partly in the doorway, and into her own cage, where she resumed her restless jumps. He was not pleased with her reception of his attentions; he sat a long time in that attitude, perfectly still, perhaps meditating what step he should take next, glancing at her meanwhile over his shoulder, but not stirring a feather. Time passed, and he came to a decision of some sort, which was shown by a change of position. He turned around, and took his seat on the corresponding perch in her cage, just before the door. This impressed Virginia; she stopped her hopping and looked over at him with an air of wondering what he would do next. What he did was to hop one step nearer, to the middle perch. Upon this she abandoned her place, came to the floor, and began to eat in the most indifferent manner; then passed into his cage, then back to the floor of her own, still eating, while he sat silent and motionless on the middle perch, evidently much disturbed by her conduct. After an hour of this performance he retired to her upper perch, and stayed there.

The same day, the jealousy of the unsuccessful wooer was aroused by a fine, fresh-looking cardinal whom he saw in the looking-glass. In flying past it he caught a glimpse of his reflection, and at once turned, alighted before it, and began calling vehemently; holding out, and quivering his wings, and flying up against the figure again and again in the most savage way. The next day he began to mope and refused to come out of the cage; whether because of illness, or disappointed affections, who shall say?

The time of her tormentor's retirement was one of great happiness to Virginia. She paid her usual visit to the robin, and he, as at first, vacated the cage, this having become the regular morning programme. Now, too, she went on to extend her acquaintance by entering the cage of another neighbor, a scarlet tanager, a shy, unobtrusive fellow, who asked nothing but to be let alone. This bird also did not reciprocate her neighborly sentiments; he met her with open beak, but finding that did not awe her, nor prevent her calmly walking in, he hastily left the cage himself. During the time that her persecutor was sulking, and not likely to bother, she had leisure for the bath, which she enjoyed freely, coming out with her long breast-feathers hanging in locks and looking like a bundle of rags. Her last experimental call was now made upon another household, the Baltimore orioles, and there she met with something new— perfect indifference. Even when both of the birds were at home they did not resent her coming in. She went to the upper perch with them; the cage was big, there was plenty of room, and they were willing. Their manners, in fact, were so agreeable that if their cups had been supplied with seed, I think she would have taken up her abode with them; as it was, she frequently spent half an hour at a time there. On this eventful day Virginia began to sing, for in her family the musical performances are not confined to the males.

After several days of retirement, the cardinal plucked up spirit to resume his annoyance of Virginia, and for a few nights a queer sort of game was played by the two, explain it who can. If the barrier between the cages was removed after the outside doors were shut for the night, he at once went to her cage and to the middle perch. Virginia, on the upper perch, waited till he reached that spot, then dropped to the floor, slipped through the door into his cage, and went to the upper perches there, where she hopped back and forth, while he did the same in her cage. Suddenly, after a few moments, down he came again through the door to his own middle perch, when instantly, as before, she retreated into her cage. Thus they went on an hour at a time; he apparently following her from one cage to another, and she declining to occupy the same apartment with him. Occasionally it was not so calm; he lost his temper, or grew tired of trying to please; once or twice, without warning, he lowered his head, looked ugly, and fairly burst into her cage and flung himself at her. She dived under or bounded over a perch, any way to escape him, and took refuge in the other cage.

This could not go on long; the cardinal lost interest in everything, took to moping, and at last died,—disappointed affection, shall we say, or what? Virginia was relieved; she sang more and in a louder tone, hopping around her cage with a seed in her mouth, flying through the room, or splashing in the bath; in fact she was bubbling over with song all the time, as if she were so happy she could not keep still. She paid her daily visits to the cages, forcing the robin to take an outing, which he did not care to do while moulting and not very sure of his powers.

Many birds show emotions by raising the feathers on different parts of the body, but this bird was remarkable in the expression of her crest alone. When she peeped into a strange cage, and was somewhat uncertain of her reception, the crest laid flat down, her very head seemed to shrink; she stepped in at the door, excited, for it might be peace and it might be war; the feathers rose and fell alternately; if suddenly startled, the crest sprang to its highest point; and when singing, or passing peacefully about the room, it dropped carelessly back on her head.

Virginia was allowed a week's solitary enjoyment of the two cages, and then one day a new tenant appeared in the cardinal's quarters. She was out in the room when he arrived, but she instantly came over and alighted on his roof, to have a look at him. Most expressive was her manner. She stood in silence and gazed upon him a long time; all her liveliness and gayety were gone, and she appeared to be struck dumb by this new complication of her affairs. It was plain that she was not pleased. Perhaps her dislike was evident to the new bird, for suddenly he flew up and snapped at her, which so surprised her that she hopped a foot into the air. When the time came to open the door into her cage, the stranger was delighted to go in, but Virginia dodged him, exactly as she had done his predecessor. He did not lose his temper and condescend to the vulgarity of flying at her, as the first admirer had done. He looked interested to see that she avoided him, but after all he did not take it much to heart. This cardinal, like the other, was not yet acclimated—if one may call it so—to life in a house, and after a week he also took his departure.

Now Virginia, free again, became at once very gay. She sang all the time; she kept the robin stirring; she bathed; she waxed fat. But her time was approaching. Spring came on, and with the first warm weather the birds began to disappear from the room. First the tanager expressed a desire to mingle with society once more, and went his way; then the orioles were sent to carry on their rough wooing in the big world outside; the robin followed; and at last Virginia was left with several big empty cages and only two birds, a reserved and solitude-loving Mexican clarin, and a saucy goldfinch, so long a captive that he had no desire for freedom. Now for the first time Virginia was lonely; the strange quiet of the once lively room worked upon her temper. She snapped at her little neighbor; she haunted the window-sill and gazed out; while nothing hindered her passage excepting the weather, our climate being rather cool for her.

At last July, with its great heat, arrived, and the restless bird was carried by a kind friend, who offered to do this good deed, to a place in Central Park, New York, where a small colony of her kind have established themselves and build and nest every year. Here she was set free, and here she met her third suitor. The place and the season were propitious, and Virginia was ready to look with favor on a smart young cardinal in the brightest of coats, who came in response to her calls the moment she found herself on a tree, really out in the world. A little coaxing, a few tender words, and she flew away with him, and we saw her no more.

FRIENDSHIP IN FEATHERS.

Why should I cumber myself with regrets that the receiver is not capacious? It never troubles the sun that some of his rays fall wide and vain into ungrateful space, and only a small part on the reflecting planet.

Emerson.

XIII.

FRIENDSHIP IN FEATHERS.

Emerson somewhere speaks of a friendship "on one side, without due correspondence on the other," and I often thought of it while watching the curious relation between two birds in my house last winter; for the more one studies our feathered neighbors, the better he comes to realize that the difference between their intelligence and that of man himself is "only of less and more."

This friendship, then, was all on one side. It was not a case of "love at sight"; on the contrary, it was first war, and the birds had been room-mates for months before any unusual interest was shown; neither was it simple admiration of beauty, for the recipient of the tenderness was at his worst at the moment; nor, again, could it be the necessity of loving somebody, for the devotee had lived in the house ten years, and had seen forty birds of almost as many kinds come and go, without exhibiting any partiality. The parties to this curious affair were, first, the beloved, a male scarlet tanager, whose summer coat was disfigured with patches of the winter dress he was trying to put on; and secondly, the lover, a male English goldfinch, scarcely half his size.

The tanager, as perhaps every one knows, is one of our most brilliant birds, bright scarlet with black wings and tail. He is as shy as he is gay, living usually in the woods, and not taking at all kindly to the enforced companionship of mankind. I had long been anxious to make the acquaintance of this retiring bird, partly because I desire to know personally all American birds, and partly because I wanted to watch his change of plumage; for the scarlet uniform is only the marriage dress, and put off at the end of the season. Hence whenever I saw a tanager in a New York bird store I brought it home, though dealers always warned me that it would not live in confinement. My first attempts were disastrous, certainly. The birds refused to become reconciled, even with all the privileges I gave them, and one after another died, I believe for no other reason than their longing for freedom. Let me say here that feeling thus, they would have received their liberty, much as I wished to study them, only their plumage was not in condition to fly, and they would go out to certain death. My hope was to make them contented through the winter, while they put on a new suit of feathers, and open the doors for them in summer.

The subject of this tale, and the last of the series, I procured of a dealer who has learned to keep tanagers in good condition, and I never had trouble with this bird's health or spirits. It was not until May that he wished to leave me. When he joined the circle in the room he had just thoroughly learned that a cage was a place he could not get out of, and he had ceased to try. The first morning when his neighbors came out of their cages he was as much astonished as if he had never seen birds out of a bird store. He stretched up and looked at them with the greatest interest. When one or two began to splash in the large shallow bathing dishes on the table, he was much excited, and plainly desired to join them. I opened his door and placed in it a long perch leading to freedom. For some time he did not come out, and when he did, the sudden liberty drove out of his head all thoughts of a bath. When he flew, he aimed straight for the trees outside the window, and of course came violently against the glass.

This experience all house birds have to go through, and it is sometimes several days before they learned the nature of glass. The tanager learned his lesson more quickly. He fell to the floor at first, from the shock, but in a few moments recovered himself and returned, this time alighting on the top of the lower sash and proceeding to examine the strange substance through which he could see, but could not go. He gently tapped the glass with his beak the whole length of the window, passing back and forth several times till satisfied. Turning at last from that, he cast his eye around for another exit, and settled on the white ceiling as the most likely place. Then he flew all about the room close to the ceiling, touched it now and then with his beak, and finding it also impassable, he came down to the window again. He had not the least curiosity about the room, and was not at all afraid of me. The world outside the windows and his cage when he was hungry, were all that he cared for at present—except the bath.

The goldfinch was bathing the second time he came out, and he went directly to the table and perched on the side of the dish. Now the one thing the little fellow most delighted in was his morning bath, and he at once resented the intrusion of the stranger. He flew at him with open beak and lifted wings, scolding vigorously, in fact gave him so hostile a reception that he quickly retired to the top of the cage, where he stood a long time. Afterward also, the goldfinch showed so strong a determination that the intruder should not enjoy his beloved bath, that at last I had to keep him in his cage while the new-comer had a chance at the water.

This did not go on long, however, for very soon the tanager deliberately gave up the world of the bird-room, and insisted on remaining in his cage. In vain was his door set open with the others, in vain did the birds splash and splatter the water, he would not come out, though he did not mope or lose his appetite. In truth, it seemed merely as if he scorned the advantages offered; if he could not go out free into the trees, he would as lief stay in his cage—and he did. This is a not uncommon habit of cage birds. They often need to be driven or coaxed out. Having once learned that the cage is home with all its comforts and conveniences, they prefer to be there.

The tanager was always a very shy bird; he did not like to be looked at. If he could manage it, he would never eat while any one saw him. Often, when I put a bit of apple or a meal-worm in his cage, he stood and looked at it and at me, but did not move till I turned away, or walked out of his sight, when he instantly pounced upon it as if starved. To make him altogether happy I put a screen around one corner of his cage, behind which were his dishes, and after that it was very droll to see him crouch behind that and eat, every moment or two stretching up to glance over the top and see if I had moved. If I stirred as though about to leave my chair, he at once whisked to the upper perch as if he had been caught in a crime.

The first I noticed of the goldfinch's friendliness to him was after he had lived with us five or six months.

This small bird, in a room of larger ones, was somewhat driven about. I do not mean hurt, but if any one wanted a certain perch he did not hesitate to take it, even if it were already occupied by so little a fellow. He soon learned that near the tanager he was not often molested, and he began first to frequent the perch that ran out of the cage—the doorstep in fact. Finding that he was not disturbed, he soon moved his quarters just inside the door. Most birds quickly resent the intrusion of another into their cage, but the tanager never did. So long as he was left alone on his favorite upper perches, he did not care who went in below. This being the case, after a while the goldfinch ventured upon the middle perch. Still he was not noticed; but presuming on the friendly attitude of his host, he one day hopped upon the perch beside him. This was a step too far; the house-owner turned an open beak toward him, and in unmistakable tones told him to leave—which he at once did, of course.

This boundary made by the tanager was never changed, but in the rest of the cage the goldfinch made himself at home, and at once assumed the position of protector. Seeing that the owner did not,—and sure it was somebody's duty,—he began to guard the door, warning away any one who wished to enter, with harsh scolding, fluttering of wings, and swelling up of his little body, amusing to see. The boldest bird in the room was awed by these demonstrations coming from the inside as though the cage were his own. The tanager looked on all this with some interest, but expressed no more gratitude at being protected than he had resentment at being driven from the bath.

Soon I noticed a certain chattering talk from the small bird that he had never indulged in excepting to another of his kind—his companion when he first came to me. It was very low but almost continuous, and was plainly addressed to the tanager. As his friendliness progressed, he found the lower perch too far from his charmer, and not being allowed to sit beside him he took to clinging upon the outside of the cage as near to the tanager's usual seat as he could get. The only perching place he had there was a band of tin that held the wires steady, but in spite of what must have been the discomfort of the position, there he hung by the hour, talking, calling, and looking at his idol within. He left the spot only to eat and bathe, and I think if the cage had been supplied with seed he would never have gone at all. When the bird inside hopped to the perch at the other end of the cage, which was the extent of his wanderings, the finch at once followed on the outside, always placing himself as near as possible. It was really touching, to all but the object of it, who took it in the most indifferent way. When the tanager went down to eat, his escort accompanied him as far as the door perch, where he stood and looked on earnestly, ready to return to his old place the moment the luncheon was finished.

On the rare occasions that the self-elected hermit went out, the goldfinch displayed great concern, evidently preferring to have his favorite at home where he could defend him. He flew uneasily across from the cage to his side, then back, as if to show him the way. He also desired to watch the empty house, to preserve it from intrusion, but was constantly divided between his duties of special porter, and bodyguard. But he did his best, even then; he followed the wanderer. If the tanager went to a perch the goldfinch at once alighted on the same, about a foot away, and sidled up as near as he was allowed. He was free to come within about three inches, but nearer he was driven off, so the little fellow placed himself at this distance and there stayed patiently as long as his friend remained. If the latter had been more responsive, I believe the goldfinch would have nestled up against him.

The tanager sometimes strayed into a strange cage, and then the anxious guard followed to the steps and even within, talking earnestly, and no doubt pointing out the danger, yet if the owner unexpectedly appeared he met him at the threshold and fiercely defended the door against the proprietor himself. Occasionally the erratic recluse went to the floor—a place never visited by his little attendant, whose trouble was almost painful to see. He at once placed himself on the lowest perch, stretched out and looked over, following every movement with his eyes, in silence, as though the danger was too great to allow conversation, and when his charge returned to a perch, he uttered a loud and joyous call as though some peril had been escaped.

The stanch little friend had many chances to show his loyalty. The other birds in the room were not slow to take advantage of one who never defended himself. In particular a Brazilian cardinal, a bold saucy fellow with a scarlet pointed crest and a loud voice, evidently considered the tanager cage common ground, open to everybody, until the goldfinch undertook its defense. It was amusing to see the small bird stand just inside, and rage, puff himself out, wave his wings, and fairly drive away the foe. So impertinent was the Brazilian that the finch declared general war upon him, and actually chased his big antagonist around the room and away from his favorite perches, hovering over his head, and flying around it in small circles, trying to peck it, till he flew away defeated, probably because he was too much amazed to think of resisting.

This was not, however, the worst enemy he had to deal with. Next door to the tanager lived a robin, a big, rollicking, fun-loving fellow who considered such a retiring personage fair game. His pleasure was to see that the tanager went out every day, and he made it his business to enforce the regulation he had set up. His tactics were to jump upon the roof of the cage, coming down violently just over the head of the tanager, who, of course, hopped quickly to the other perch. Then the robin began a mad war-dance across the cage, wings held up, tail spread, bill clattering, and altogether looking as full of mischief as any bad boy one ever saw, while the tanager went wild below, flying in a panic back and forth, but not for some time thinking of leaving the cage. The instant this performance began, the little champion was upon him; he alighted at one end of the short tramping ground on the cage, and met his big foe with open beak and every sign of war. The robin simply lowered his head and went for him, and the little bird had to fly. He pluckily returned at once to the other end and faced him again.

Observing that the goldfinch alone was not able to keep the robin away, I provided the cage with a roof of paper, which is usually a perfect protection, since birds dislike the rustle. It did not dismay this naughty fellow, however; on the contrary, it gave an added zest because of that very quality. He pranced across it in glee, making a great noise, and when the violence of his movements pushed it aside, he peered down on the tanager, who stood panting. The sight pleased him, and he resumed his pranks; he lifted the handle of the cage and let it drop with a clatter; he jerked off bits of paper and dropped them into the cage, and in every way showed a very mischievous spirit. Meanwhile, all through the confusion the goldfinch scolded furiously, flying around to get a peck at him, and in every way challenging him to fight. Occasionally, when he became too troublesome, the robin turned and snapped his beak at him, but did not choose to leave the bigger game.

When at last he tired of his fun, or was driven away, the goldfinch flew to the side of the cage where the frightened tanager had taken refuge, though there was not even a strip of tin to hold on, uttered his loud cheerful call several times, plainly congratulating and reassuring him, and telling him all was safe; and here he clung with difficulty to the upright wires, all the time slipping down, till the tanager went to the upper regions again. Every time the robin so much as flew past, the tireless little fellow rushed out at him, scolding. When finally the robin went into his own cage, and the tanager returned to his usual place, the goldfinch at once assumed his uncomfortable perch and sang a loud sweet song, wriggling his body from side to side, and expressing triumph and delight in a remarkable way.

The approach of spring made a change in the tanager. He had not so completely given up the world as it appeared. He began to chirp, to call, and at last to sing. He was still so shy he went down behind his screen to sing, but sing he must and did. Now, too, he began to resent the attentions of his admirer, occasionally giving the poor little toes a nip, as they clung to the tin band near his seat. He also went out now, and turned an open beak upon his friend. From simply enduring him, he suddenly began offensive operations against him. Poor little lover! an ungrateful peck did not drive him away, but simply made him move a little farther off, and stopped his gentle twittering talk a while. But the tanager grew more and more belligerent. He came out every day, took soaking baths, and returned to his examination of the windows, for the trees were green outside, and plainly he longed to be on them. He stood and looked out, and called, and held his wings up level with his back, fluttering them gently.

All this time the devotion of the little one never changed, though it was so badly received. When the tanager turned savagely and gave his faithful friend a severe peck, instead of resenting it the hurt bird flew to another perch, where he stood a long time, uttering occasionally a low, plaintive call, as if of reproach, all his cheerfulness gone, a melancholy sight indeed. I waited only for warm days to set free the tanager, and at last they came. Early in June the bird was put into a traveling cage, carried into the country, where a lovely bit of woods and a pretty lake insured a good living, and the absence of sparrows made it safe for a bird that had been caged. Then the door was opened, and he instantly flew out of sight.

The bird left at home seemed a little lost for a few days, moped about, often visited the empty cage, but in a short time entirely abandoned it, and evidently looked no more for his friend. But he is changed too: not quite so gay as before; not so much singing; and not a word of the soft chattering talk we heard so constantly while his beloved friend was here.

THE ROSY SHIELD.

Soft falls his chant as on the nest
Beneath the sunny zone,
For love that stirred it in his breast

Has not aweary grown,
And 'neath the city's shade can keep
The well of music clear and deep.
And love that keeps the music, fills
With pastorial memories.
All echoing from out the hills,
All droppings from the skies,
All flowings from the wave and wind
Remembered in the chant I find.
Elizabeth Barrett Browning.

XIV.

THE ROSY SHIELD.

One of the most winning inhabitants of my bird-room last winter bore on his snow-white breast a pointed shield of beautiful rose-color, and the same rich hue lined his wings. With these exceptions his dress was of sober black and white, though so attractively disposed that he was an extremely pretty bird—the rose-breasted grosbeak.

Nor was beauty his only attraction; he was a peculiar character, in every way different from his neighbors. He was dignified, yet his dignity was not like that of a thrush; he was calm and cool, yet not after the manner of an orchard oriole. He possessed a lovely gentleness of disposition, and a repose of manner unparalleled among my birds. Vulgar restlessness was unknown to him; flying about for mere exercise, or hopping from perch to perch to pass away time, he scorned. The frivolous way common to smaller birds of going for each seed as they want it, was beneath him. When he wished to eat he did so like a civilized being, that is, took his stand by the seed-cup, and stayed there, attending strictly to the business in hand till he had finished, leaving a neat pile of canary-seed shells in one spot, instead of the general litter common to cages. The meal over, he was ready to go out of the cage, place himself comfortably in one of his favorite corners, and remain for a long time, amused with the life in the room and the doings in the street, on both of which he seemed to look with the eye of a philosopher. In the same deliberate and characteristic way he disposed of a meal-worm, or a bit of beef, which he enjoyed. He never bolted it outright like a thrush, nor beat it to death like a tanager, nor held it under one toe and took it in mouthfuls like an oriole: he quietly worked it back and forth between his mandibles till reduced to a pulp, and then swallowed it.

The rosy shield-bearer was preëminently a creature of habit. Very early in his life with us he selected certain resting places for his private use, and all the months of his stay he never changed them. The one preferred above all others was the middle bar of the window-sash, in the corner, and I noticed that his choice was always a corner. In this sunny spot he spent most of the time, closely pressed against the window-casing, generally looking out at the trees and the sparrow-life upon them, and regarding every passer-by in the street, not in an unhappy way, but apparently considering the whole a panorama for his entertainment. When events in the room interested him, his post of observation was a bracket that held a small cage, where he often sat an hour at a time in perfect silence, looking at everybody, concerned about everything, his rosy shield and white breast effectively set off by the dark paper behind him.

Although thus immobile and silent, the grosbeak was far from being stupid. He had decided opinions and tastes as well defined as anybody's. For example, when he came to me his cage stood on a shelf next to that occupied by two orchard orioles, and he was never pleased with the position. He was hardly restless even there, while suffering what he plainly considered a grievance, but he was uneasy. I saw that something was wrong, and guessed at once that it was because his upper perch was three inches lower than that in the next cage, and to have a neighbor higher than himself is always an offense to a bird. As soon as I raised his cage he was satisfied on that score, and no more disturbed me in the early morning by shuffling about on his perch and trying to fly upward.

But still things were not quite to his mind, and he showed it by constantly going into the cage of the orioles and settling himself evidently with the desire of taking up his residence there. He was so gentle and unobtrusive everywhere, that no one resented his presence in the cage, and he could have lived in peace with almost any bird. But I wanted him contented at home, and moreover, I was curious to find out what was amiss, so I tried the experiment of removing his cage from its position next to the lively orioles, and hanging it alone between two windows, where, although not so light, it had the advantage of solitude. The change completed the happiness of the grosbeak. From that day he no more intruded upon others, but went and came freely and joyously to his own cage, and from being hard to catch at night he became one of the most easy, proceeding the moment he entered his home toward dark to the upper perch to wait for me to close the door before going to his seed-dish. In fact, he grew so contented that he cared little to come out, and often sat in his favorite corner of the cage by the hour, with the door wide open and the other birds flying around. Now, too, he began to sing in a sweet voice a very low and tender minor strain.

Among his other peculiarities this bird scarcely ever seemed to feel the need of utterance of any soft. On the rare occasions of any excitement he delivered a sharp, metallic "click"; a sudden alarm, like the attack of another bird, called out a war-cry loud and shrill, and very odd; and in the contest over the important question of precedence at the bath he sometimes uttered a droll squeal or whining sound. Besides these, he made singular noises in bathing and dressing his feathers, which are not uncommon among birds, but are difficult to describe. They always remind me of the rubbing of machinery in need of oil.

This beautiful bird was not easily frightened; the only time I ever saw him seriously disturbed was at the sight of a stuffed screech-owl, which I brought into the room without thinking of its probable effect. I placed it on a shelf in a closet, and I soon noticed that the moment the closet door was opened the grosbeak became greatly agitated; he darted across the room to a certain retreat where he always hurried on the first alarm of any sort, and remained in retirement till the fancied danger was over, while the others flew madly about.

In this place he stood posturing in much excitement, and uttering at short intervals his sharp "click." For some time I did not understand his conduct, nor think of connecting it with the owl on the shelf; but when it did occur to me I tried the experiment of bringing it out into the room, when I immediately saw, what I should have remembered at once, that it was an object of terror to all the birds.

The song of the rose-breasted grosbeak is celebrated, and I hoped my bird would become acquainted with us, and let out his voice; but I was disappointed in both respects, for he never became familiar in the least, and though not at all afraid he was very shy; and furthermore, upon my bringing into the room two small musical thrushes, the grosbeak—feeling, as I said, no need of utterance— readily relapsed into silence, and all the winter never sang a note. His conduct before the looking-glass indicated that he was not naturally so silent, and that he could be social with one who understood his language. Being unable to get another grosbeak, I tried to give him companionship by placing a small glass against one end of his cage. On seeing his reflection the bird was greatly agitated, began his low, whining cry, postured, bowed, turned, moved back and forth, and at last left the cage and looked for the stranger behind the glass. Not finding him he returned, had another interview with the misleading image, and ended as before in seeking him outside. At length he seemed to be convinced that there was something not quite natural about it, for, feeling hungry, he went, with many a backward glance at the glass, to the floor, took a hemp-seed and carried it out into the room to eat, a thing he never did at any other time.

I spoke of my bird's posturing; that was one of his pleasures, and almost his only exercise while he lived in the house. He was not graceful, his body was not flexible, and his tail was far from being the expressive member it is with many birds, it always stood straight out; he could raise it with a little jerk, and he had a beautiful way of opening it like a fan, but I never saw it droop or stir in any other way. In these movements his head and tail maintained the same relative position to the body, as though they were cut out of one piece of wood; but he bowed and leaned far over on one side, with his short legs wide spread; he passed down a perch, alternately crouching and rising, either sideways or straight; he jerked his whole body one side and then the other, in a manner ludicrously suggestive of a wriggle; he sidled along his perch, holding his wings slightly out and quivering, then slowly raised them both straight up, and instantly dropped them, or held them half open, fluttering and rustling his feathers.

He had also a curious way of moving over a long perch: he proceeded by sidewise hops, and at each hop he turned half round, that is, the first step he faced the window, the next the room, the third the window again, and so on to the end, coming down at every jump as though he weighed a pound or two. He was much addicted to sitting with breast-feathers puffed out covering his toes, or sometimes with wings held a little way from his body, showing the delicate rose-colored lining, as though conscious how pretty he looked; and among other eccentric habits he often thrust out his tongue, first one side and then the other, apparently to clean his bill.

Bathing and getting dry was conducted by this peculiar bird in a manner characteristic of himself. Slow to make the plunge, he was equally deliberate in coming out of the bath. When fairly in, he first thrust his head under, then sat up in the drollest way, head quite out of water and tail lying flat on the bottom, while he spattered vigorously with wings and tail. When he stepped out, the bath was over; he never returned for a second dip, but passed at once to a favorite corner of the window-bar, and stood there a most disconsolate-looking object, shivering with cold, with plumage completely disheveled, but making not the least effort to dry his feathers for several minutes. If the sun shone, he indulged himself in a sunning, erecting the feathers of his chin till he looked as if he wore a black muffler, opening his tail like a fan, spreading and crossing his wings over the back. This attitude made a complete change in his looks, showing white where black should be, and *vice versa*. This was the result of his peculiar coloring. Next the skin all feathers were the common slate-color, but outside of that each feather was black and white. On the back the black was at the tip, and the white between that and the slate-color; on the breast this order was reversed, and the white at the tip. Thus when wet the white and black were confused, and he resembled an object in patch-work. The rose-colored shield was formed by the slightest possible tips of that color on the white ends, and it was wonderful that they should arrange themselves in an unbroken figure, with a sharply defined outline, for each feather must have lain in its exact place to secure the result.

The different ways in which birds greet advancing night has long been a subject of interest to me, some restless and nervous, others calm, and a few wild and apparently frightened. In no one thing is there more individuality of action, and in my room that winter were exhibited every evening quite a variety of methods. A brown thrush or thrasher on the approach of darkness became exceedingly restless, flying about his cage, going over and under and around his perches, posturing in extraordinary ways, uttering at every moment a strange, harsh-breathing sound. Two smaller thrushes met the evening hour by fluttering, and a queer sort of dance elsewhere described. Two orchard orioles saluted the twilight by gymnastics on the roof of the cage. The bluebirds made careful and deliberate arrangements for a comfortable night, while the grosbeak differed from all in simply fluffing himself out, and settling himself, on the first hint of dark, in the chosen corner, whence he scarcely moved, and as soon as objects grew indistinct he laid his head quietly in its feather pillow and stirred no more. The brightest gaslight an hour later did not disturb him; if a noise wakened him, he simply looked up to see what was the matter, but did not move, and soon turned back to his rest, when slight jerks of his wings, and faint complaining sounds, told that he not only slept, but dreamed.

The bearer of the rosy shield was a persistent individual; having once taken a notion into his head, nothing would make him forget it or change his mind. Fully settled in his preference for a certain perch on the window, the coldest day in winter, with the wind blowing a gale through the crack between the sashes, would not make him desert it. Driving him away from the spot had not the slightest effect on him, he returned the moment he was left in peace. Thinking that another cage was more convenient for his use, nothing short of absolute shutting the door would keep him out of it. Nor did he forget about it either; if the door was accidentally left open, after being closed for weeks, he entered as quickly as though he had been in every day.

This bird never showed any playfulness of disposition; indeed, he had too much dignity to do so. He never flew around the room as though he liked to use his wings, although they were perfect, and there was nothing to prevent if he chose. Nor did he display curiosity about his surroundings. The only things he appeared to notice were the doings of the birds and people in the room, and the moving panorama without, which latter he always viewed with equanimity, although the sound of a hand-organ aroused him to a sort of mild fury.

As spring advanced, the beautiful grosbeak grew tuneful and often added his exquisite song to the rippling music of the small thrushes, and—with a little stretch of the imagination as to its duration—

"Trilled from out his carmine breast,

His happy breast, the livelong day."

THE BIRD OF MYSTERY.

For me there is a mystery unrevealed;

Sweet Nature, speak to me!

Lucy Larcom.

XV.

THE BIRD OF MYSTERY.

It is well that Nature has so carefully guarded the lives of her most beautiful birds, for it is a sad fact that, in the words of an eminent writer, "the winged order—the loftiest, the tenderest, the most sympathetic with man—is that which man nowadays pursues most cruelly." Had they been as accessible as sparrows, even although they equaled them in numbers, not one would by this time be alive on earth.

The family whose extraordinary dress and mystery of origin justify its name—Birds of Paradise—is securely hidden in distant islands not friendly to bird-hunting races. Inaccessible mountains and pathless forests repel the traveler; impassable ravines bar his advance; sickness and death lie in wait for the white man, while the native lurks with poisoned dart behind every bush.

The first of the race that came to us were heralded by myth and invested with marvels: they had no feet; they slept upon the wing; they fed upon dew, and hatched their eggs upon their backs. Such were the tales that accompanied the skins, magnificent beyond anything known to the world in the glory of plumage, and they were named Birds of Paradise. But science is supposed in these days to conquer all mysteries, and science armed itself with powder and shot, game bags, provision trains, and servants, and set out for the far-away inhospitable islands, the home of this, the most attractive of all. Science has solved many problems: the "Heart of Africa" has become a highway; the Polar sea and the source of the Nile are no longer unknown; but with her most persistent efforts during three hundred years she has not yet been able to give us the life history of this one feathered family. Many of her devotees have penetrated to its home and brought back fresh varieties; money, health, and life have been freely spent; but, save for a few strange and curious facts, we know little more of the manner of life of the Birds of Paradise than we did when we depended on the native legends. How some of them look we know; we have their skins wired into shape in our museums and gorgeously pictured in our books; but every traveler finds new kinds, and how many sorts there may be which have so far eluded the few and short visits of naturalists, no one is able to tell. Even of those we have, how scanty is our knowledge! What they eat we are told; how they bathe and dress their plumage; their loud calls and unmusical voices; the shyness of those whose conspicuous beauty sets a price upon their heads, and their "dancing parties," so graphically described by Wallace; but of their nesting we are in profound ignorance. Where the gravely dressed partners of the brilliant creatures set up the hearthstone none can tell, unless it be the mop-headed Papuan, and he will not.

The colors lavished on the plumage would alone make the Birds of Paradise the wonder of the world; exquisite tints not surpassed by the humming-birds themselves, and of almost infinite variety, from the richest velvety purple to the gorgeous metallic greens, blues, and yellows, changing with every motion, and glittering in the sun like gems. But the marvelous freaks in the arrangement of the plumage are more specially interesting. So extraordinary a variety of forms, so unique and fantastic in disposal, are without parallel in the animal world. Some species are adorned with long, drooping tufts of plumes light as air, as the Red Bird of Paradise, and others bear strange-shaped, movable shields; part of the family wear ruffs, and others display fans on shoulders or breast; a few sport extravagant length of tail, and one or two show bright-hued wattles; one species is bare-headed, and—other vagaries being exhausted—two have curls. The greater number have an unusual development of two or more feathers into long, wire-like objects, with a patch of web at the ends. In one species these wires are formed into two perfect circles beyond the end of the tail; in another they cross each other in a graceful double curve, and in a third stand straight and stiff from the end of the feathers. The Sexpennis, or Golden Bird of Paradise, has on the head six of these shafts, which it erects at pleasure, producing a singular appearance; and the Standard Wing has two on each wing, equally effective. Perhaps the most peculiar fact about the family is the power each bird possesses to change its form by means of these eccentric ornaments. All are erectile and movable in several ways, and a bird that is at one moment like our common crow in shape, may in the next show a dazzling array of waving plumes or vibrating fans, and be utterly unrecognizable for the same creature. It is evident to all bird students that feathers are as surely an "index of the mind" as are tails in cat and dog, and the manners and expression of this family would be a study of absorbing interest.

Not to mention the birds already familiar in books, there are a few interesting peculiarities of some of the late discoveries, and the possible varieties are by no means exhausted, so that each new traveler who penetrates into their chosen home will doubtless have opportunity to see his own name Latinized into dignity and bestowed upon some brilliant and hitherto unknown bird, having a new disposition of plumage, or a color more beautiful—if conceivable—than any before. One of the most attractive of the recent additions to the list was made by Signor D'Albertis, and named for him *Drepanoris Albertisi*. In a letter to a Sydney newspaper he tells the story of the discovery, which occurred while he was living in a Papuan mansion built upon the trunks of trees, and reached by means of a long ladder. From this unique residence he made excursions into the mountains, and, among other things, had the good fortune to see two curious episodes in the life of the Six-shafted Bird of Paradise. He found this bird—which is not new to science—to be a noisy and solitary fellow, roaming the thick woods alone, dining upon figs and other fruits, and indulging in the strange habit of "dusting" itself like a city sparrow. Happily he saw the whole operation. Selecting a suitable spot, the beautiful bird first cleared away the grass and leaves, and while the eager observer was wondering what all this preparation portended, suddenly flung itself to the ground, and rolled its rich plumage in the dust, fluttered the wings, elevated and depressed the six plumes on its head, and otherwise appeared to enjoy itself extremely. At another time the traveler witnessed a second uncommon scene in the deep interior of the forest. A bird of the same species alighted upon the ground, and after peering in every direction, either to make sure of being unobserved, or to discover an enemy or a friend, began a most singular performance, waving the six long plumes of the head, raising and lowering a small tuft of silvery white feathers over its beak, elevating a glittering crest on its neck, and spreading and drawing back the long feathers on its sides, every movement entirely changing its apparent shape. In a short time it began to jump from side to side and to assume an attitude of war, and all the time it never ceased uttering an uncommon note, as though calling for admiration or for a fight.

Not long after this curious exhibition followed the observer's great prize, the *Drepanoris Albertisi*, which is so rare that even to many of the natives it was a surprise. At the first glance this bird does not appear to deserve a place in the remarkable family. It is about the size of our common crow, brown on the back and lavender-gray below, with a curved bill more than three inches long. But closer study reveals several peculiarities: a bare space of bright blue around the eye, brilliant green on the throat, and a pair of feathery tufts standing up on the forehead like horns, with the crowning attraction of two pairs of fans, one behind the other on each side of the breast, capable of being folded smoothly against the body, or spread wide in two gorgeous semicircles altering the entire outlines of the creature. The first of the two admirable ornaments, when in repose, appears of the same violet-gray hue as the breast; but when raised the bases of the feathers are seen to be of a brilliant red, giving the effect of longitudinal stripes. The second pair is much longer, with deep margins of splendid purple instead of the stripes. When the possessor of all this splendor spreads its four fans, it also erects the long tail and opens it widely into a fifth fan, which produces an astonishing effect.

Another of D'Albertis's contributions to the mysterious family is among its most magnificent members, the *Paradisea Raggiana*. A fine specimen of this genus, mounted in the position described by Wallace as the "dancing" attitude of *P. Apoda*, the floating plumes elevated in a "golden glory" above the head, is the gem of the collection in the American Museum of New York. It resembles the Great Bird of Paradise, having long, airy plumes springing from under each wing. In general color golden brown, with yellow head and green throat. To this bird, as to others, beauty is a dangerous possession; and, as if feeling aware of the fact, it lives in the tops of tall trees, in the deepest forest, among the most inaccessible ravines. But wary though it be, one characteristic lures it to destruction—curiosity. A European hunter in his unfamiliar dress is an irresistible attraction; nearer and nearer it comes, hopping from branch to branch, pausing at every step to observe and study the intruder, with neck stretched and wings flapping, every moment uttering a peculiar cry, no doubt equivalent to "Come and look!" for it brings others upon the scene, till the pretty sight is rudely ended by a shot and a death-wound. The cry of distress brings the friends nearer, only to fall victims in their turn to the same murderous gun. Our traveler once surprised a female of this species, and a droll proceeding followed. After flying several times around his head to see what sort of a creature he might be, she alighted on a vine, and turning heels over head, remained hanging head down, sharply scrutinizing his appearance from this point of view till he—shot her.

A bare-headed bird would not seem to present any attraction to the lover of beauty, though it might be of scientific interest; but Nature, not having exhausted her resources upon the Birds of Paradise already mentioned, has even accomplished the feat of making a bald-headed beauty. The bare skin on the whole crown is of a brilliant blue color most oddly crossed by narrow rows of minute feathers, which irresistibly remind one of the sutures of the human skull. That color shall not be lacking, it bears, besides the blue of the head, black, straw color, bright red, and green; and is further adorned with two very long central tail feathers, which reach far beyond the rest of the tail, and return, making a complete circle; a rare and lovely ornament. A good specimen is among the later arrivals at the American Museum.

The *Manucodia* are the curly Birds of Paradise, and our knowledge of one of the latest and most novel of them is owing not to the indefatigable naturalists who have braved the dangers and discomfort of their wild island home, neither to the English Wallace, the Dutch Von Rosenburg, the Italian Beccari, nor to D'Albertis, nor Bruiju, nor De Myer, whose names will be forever associated with the splendid family, but to a British officer of scientific tastes.

M. Comrii is the largest, and has more curls than any other yet discovered, for they not only decorate the top of the head, but extend down the neck, and form ridges over the eyes. Even the tail partakes of the general curve, which makes it boat-shaped, and—most fantastic of all—the two middle feathers are nearly an inch shorter than their next neighbors, and turned over at the ends so as to display the different color of their inner surface, and form what ladies call "*revers.*"

"Such eccentricities are really not to be accounted for, as we cannot conceive they can be for any useful purpose" (!), gravely says science in the person of an English authority. This severely disapproved of plumage is blue with green lights on back and head, and black edged on every feather, with purple on the breast.

Another species of the curly family, the Blue-green Paradise Bird (*M. Chalybea*), has been known to us for a hundred years, but its habits are as much a mystery as its curls. It is exquisite in color, of the richest purple, glossy as satin, with neck of deep green, and all crinkled and curled over head and neck.

The Long-tailed Bird of Paradise is the proud possessor of twenty-two names, from which it were hard to make a selection. It is one of the largest, being twenty-two inches in length, most of which, however, is tail, and is splendid in soft velvet-like black with hints of green and blue and purple. On each side it carries a fan of curved feathers, and the plumes of the flanks are of the lightest and most delicate texture. Words cannot describe the grace and elegance of this bird, and the perfect specimen in the museum above mentioned is worthy of a pilgrimage to see.

A "changeable" Bird of Paradise is the one remaining eccentricity conceivable to complete the variety in coloring, and this is found in the *Epimachus Ellioti,* a bird so rare that at the time Gould published his first work the specimen in his collection was unique, and naturalists in their excursions in the Papuan Islands have vainly tried to discover its home and learn its habits. The whole incomparable plumage is of rich changeable hues; in ordinary light, when perfectly motionless, the bird appears of a soft black, but on moving about the color varies from violet to maroon, from this to deep amethyst, and then to green, purple, and blue. A most extraordinary effect is produced when it faces the spectator with fan-plumes expanded, reaching so far above its head that they look like a pair of arms thrown up.

The most interesting though not the most beautiful of the family is the Gardener bird, discovered a few years ago by the Italian naturalist Beccari. Here is a Bird of Paradise eccentric not in dress but in habits. His plumage is modest brown in several shades, so inconspicuous that the partner of his joys can wear the same tints, which she does. The bird is the size of a turtle-dove. Let the doctor himself tell the story of the discovery while walking through the beautiful forest, so thick that scarcely a ray of sunshine penetrated the branches. He says:

"I suddenly stood before the most remarkable specimen of the industry of an animal. It was a hut or bower close to a small meadow enameled with flowers. The whole was on a diminutive scale, and I immediately recognized the famous nests described by the hunters of Bruiju. After well observing the whole I gave strict orders to my hunters not to destroy the little building. That, however, was an unnecessary caution, since the Papuans take great care never to disturb these nests or bowers, even if they are in their way. The birds had evidently enjoyed the greatest quiet until we happened, unfortunately for them, to come near them. I had now full employment in the preparation of my treasure.... I took colors and brushes, and went to the spot, and made the sketch which I now publish. When I was there neither host nor hostess was at home.... I could not ascertain whether this bower was occupied by one pair or more, whether the male alone is the builder, or whether the wife assists. I believe, however, that the nest lasts several seasons."

The pleasing description of the house and lawn, with its many decorations, has been widely copied. "Being mostly near the entrance," says the grave scientist in conclusion, surprised into sentiment, "it would appear that the husband offers there the daily gift to the wife, removing the objects to the back of the hut as they fade or wither." It is clever not only in building a house and lawn, but in imitating the songs and cries of other birds, and doing it so well, according to our author, that it brought "his hunters to despair."

So few Birds of Paradise have entered the scientific world alive, and so little is known of their manners, that the meagre accounts we have possess unusual interest. So long ago as early in the century Mr. Bennett, in his visit to Macao, wrote a statement of the ways of a Great Bird of Paradise (*P. Apoda*) which had been at that time in confinement nine years. His description of the toilet of the most exquisite of birds is delightful.

"It washes itself regularly twice daily, and after having performed its ablutions, throws its delicate feathers up nearly over the head.... The beautiful subalar plumage is then thrown out and cleaned from any spot that may sully its purity by being passed gently through the bill, the short chocolate-colored wings are extended to the utmost, and he keeps them in a steady flapping motion, at the same time raising up the delicate long feathers over the back, which are spread in a chaste and elegant manner, floating like films in the ambient air. In this position the bird would remain for a short time, seemingly proud of its heavenly beauty. I never yet beheld a soil on its feathers. After expanding the wings it would bring them together so as to conceal the head, then bending gracefully it would inspect the state of its plumage underneath.... It then picks and cleans its plumage in every part within reach, and throwing out the elegant and delicate tuft of feathers underneath, they are cleaned in succession, if required, by throwing them abroad, elevating and passing them in succession through the bill. Then turning its back to the spectators, the actions above mentioned are repeated, ... and throwing its feathers up with much grace, appears as proud as a lady dressed in her full ball dress"(!). After further account of its taking grasshoppers from visitors, he concludes: "Should any of the insects fall to the floor of his cage he will not descend to them, appearing to be fearful that in so doing he should soil his delicate plumage."

Almost equally charming is Mr. Bennett's observation of one that Wallace carried alive to London, which lived two years there and became exceedingly tame. It is this species whose dancing parties Wallace thus describes:—

"On one of these trees a dozen or twenty full-plumaged male birds assemble, raise their wings vertically over the back, stretch out their necks, and raise and expand their exquisite long plumes till they form two magnificent golden fans, which are kept in continual vibration. Between whiles they fly across from branch to branch in great excitement, so that the whole tree is filled with waving plumes in every variety of attitude and motion. In the position above mentioned the whole bird is overshadowed by his plumage, the crouching body, yellow head, and emerald green throat form but the foundation and setting to the golden glory which waves above. Seen in this attitude the Bird of Paradise really deserves its name, and must be ranked as one of the most beautiful and most wonderful of living things."

In truth, it is so transcendently beautiful that hunters have been astonished into forgetfulness of their guns, and no triumph was ever greater, for to recognize an attractive creature and lift the gun to take its life seems to be a single operation of many who carry the murderous weapon.

The Twelve-wired, one of the better known varieties of the Birds of Paradise, is usually figured, and probably always mounted, with its exquisite plumes closely folded against its sides, but the French naturalist and traveler Le Vaillant, in his large work published early in the century, gives a representation of it under the name of *Le Nebuleux*, with feathers expanded to the uttermost, a truly magnificent display. All his figures, though sometimes incorrect, owing to the scanty knowledge of the time, have a great deal of life. Each bird is presented both in repose, with plumage all folded smoothly back, and in excitement, with every fan and ruff and erectile ornament fully spread.

This peerless family takes kindly to captivity, as has been amply proved by their enduring the voyage and living two years in the unfavorable climate of England, as well as by spending at least nine years in an aviary in China, and there is no reason why we in America should not have opportunity to admire them and study their habits from life. Would that some of our young explorers could be induced to turn from the ice-fields of the Poles, and the death-swamps of the Tropics, to seek these inimitable birds in the mountains and woods of the Papuan Islands—not to shoot for our museum shelves, but to study their manners and customs, and above all to introduce them into American aviaries, that a new and absorbing chapter might be added to our Natural Histories, and the Bird of Paradise cease to be the Bird of Mystery.